MILK, MUCK AND MEMORIES

FARMING LIVES COLLECTED BY MARGARET WOMBWELL

Derbyshire County Council
Cultural & Community Services Department
2007

Published by Derbyshire County Council Cultural and Community Services Department, County Hall, Matlock, DE4 3AG 2007

ISBN 978 0 903463 84 3

This book is compiled from tape recordings of conversations between Margaret Wombwell and the contributors made between 2003 and 2007. There are also written recollections from a few individuals. All the original tape recordings are held at the Local Studies Library, County Hall, Matlock.

The opinions of the interviewees are their own and not necessarily those of Derbyshire County Council.

ACKNOWLEDGEMENTS
The illustrations are provided by kind permission of many generous people including A. Knighton, G. Else, J. Hollingworth, A. Hind, W.D. Woodall, P. Marsden, J. Ravey, S. Band, J. Hopkinson, M. Taylor, M. Hardwick, D. Wombwell, S. Sloan of the Nettle Inn, Milltown, H.V. Green.
Page 157 by courtesy of Nottinghamshire County Council
Pages 127, 131 by courtesy of Derby Museums and Art Gallery
Page 96 by courtesy Peter Johnson, Thornhill House
The remainder are from library collections and www.picturethepast.org.uk

Thanks to Mrs M. Graney for permission to use Ted Hellaby's paintings and diary. Mrs M. Brailsford for photographs and account book of Hilltop Farm. H. Davison for photographs and farm accounts. Mrs K. Brailsford for Ashover Show material. Dr. Jennifer James for original sketches on pages 30, 69.

A NOTE ABOUT WEIGHTS, MEASURES AND CURRENCY.
The memories in this book all precede the change to metric measurements and decimal currency so the speakers use the terminology of the time. So that the reader today can have an understanding of the amounts being quoted some comparisons are given.

1 yard = 0.914 metres
1 foot = 30.48 centimetres
1 inch = 2.54 centimetres
1 hundredweight = 50.8 kilograms
1 pound = 0.4536 kilograms
1 ounce = 28.35 grams
£1 = 20 shillings or 240 old pence
5 new pence = 1 shilling or 12 old pence
1 new penny = 2.4 old pence

Designed by: Dick Richardson, Country Books. Little Longstone.
Printed and bound by: Whittington Moor Printing Works Ltd., Chesterfield

CONTENTS

INTRODUCING... THE
CONTRIBUTORS AND THEIR FARMS

"As long as he's got two hands and two feet,
that's all that matters to me."

So one farmer summed up his requirements of a farm lad beginning work. The land itself, and the men and women who farmed it, are the characters in this story. The land was not always hospitable to these people who worked, and in some cases still work it. The memories in this book come from farming people in the area between Matlock and Chesterfield, particularly around Ashover Their depth of experience and complete dedication provide a vivid picture of what it means to have been a part of the Derbyshire countryside through the 20th century.

The contributors introduce themselves, beginning with the oldest, **Miss Elizabeth Bassett**, who died in 2004 aged 101.

Miss Bassett recalls working on the family farm at Hilltop, Ashover, in particular during the war. "My youngest brother was the farmer, he was older than me. He was, well, you'd call it apprenticed to a farm and unfortunately he got killed in a motor-bicycle accident when he was 18 or 19. My father wanted to carry on the farm so he put in a farm manager. Then I came home from boarding school, and I followed on and did a bit of farming. My war effort was farm work. I was in the Women's Land Army and went round to shows and that sort of thing."

Mavis Brailsford was married to the Bassetts' farm manager. Her husband's account book and photographs have pro-vided most interesting material highlighting the day to day work-

Hilltop Farm 1927. It was the Bassetts' custom to walk round the farm on Sunday mornings. From the left: John Bassett, Bernard Brailsford, his farm manager, Miss B. Overton and Miss Bassett herself on the right.

ing of a farm. She and her brother John Hodgson were born in Ashover, the children of Alan Hodgson. The family had a dairy and delivered milk as well as running a taxi cab business on Moor Road. During the war John worked on an experimental farm at Gladwin Mark for the Ministry of Agriculture.

Fred and Ethel Hole have farmed at several places including Lea Hall Farm where they had a herd of Red Polls. For a number of years Mr Hole worked as a travelling salesman for Baileys, the corn merchants, at Matlock. **Mrs Dorothy Ward** also lived at Lea Hall where her family, her father, grandfather, and great uncle James, farmed for 19 years. Before they moved there, when she was about ten, they farmed Walnut Farm,

Brackenfield on the Turbutt estate. Dorothy has been at her present home, Woolley Farm, for over 50 years.

Also from Woolley, **Bert Hopkinson** wrote memories of his young life at Revel Farm, Woolley in the 1920s and 30s and **Harry Towndrow** lived at Woolley Moor. **Mrs Ellen Eaton** was born in Woolley but has lived in Ashover since 1928. She and her daughter in law, **Betty Dimbleby**, fondly remember their family pigs. Another proud pig owner is **Mrs Roma Unwin**. She came to Ashover in 1947 when she was 17. People said she wouldn't stop because there were so few young people but stop she did, working in the family shop ever since.

Millie Ablett (née Tomlinson) was born and brought up on Sycamore Farm in Littlemoor. Although Littlemoor is quite separate from Ashover the family felt very much a part of that village, a feeling strengthened because they went to school there. "In my very early days, my dad's family (he was a Tomlinson from the Black Swan) used to taxi people to the station with horses. At

The Tomlinsons with one of their taxis outside the Black Swan, Ashover.

one time they had 20 or so horses. They took mail too, to Chesterfield and Sheffield. They used to call it "Maily." They were undertakers too. The hearse finished up at Sycamore farm. We used to play in it as children. There were quite a lot of young children at Littlemoor, big families, and they all seemed to congregate at the farm. Some came to work and some came to play. In 1948 I got married, to the boy next door you might say, because he worked on the farm that used to do the binding. He used to work the binder so we fell in love over the fence, not the garden wall. I didn't move very far. When I got married we went to Handley."

Mrs Eva Butler joined Millie Ablett to contribute her memories. She too grew up in Littlemoor where her grandparents had a smallholding. She has fond memories of their work and of the Tomlinsons' farm at the other end of the village. Also from Littlemoor, **Margaret Graney** was born in what had originally been a gamekeeper's cottage. It had no electricity, only gas downstairs and a candle or a torch to take you to bed. When her grandfather died, Margaret and her family moved up the hill to Home Farm, Littlemoor. Her father, **Ted Hellaby**, kept a diary and enjoyed painting and drawing. Extracts from his diary and a number of his delightful pictures illustrate this book.

Violet Gascoyne, was also born in Littlemoor but grew up in Alton. She has some interesting reminiscences of farming life in that village. **Hilda Hopkinson** (neé Taylor) spent her childhood in Alton too and helped on the local farms. **Lily Barker**, (née Fearn) lived at nearby Northedge in the 1940s and has fond memories of the farms around her home.

Colin Marriott was born at Church Farm, Temple Normanton, in 1922. "The farm we lived on, they've made that all into houses. It was a grand village, that was. There was farm here, and just a few yards, there were school. You could soon run up and down. We were surrounded with farms up at that end, small farms. We left that farm, because it were a family farm and they sold it. Then we come down to Williamthorpe. We hadn't been down there long – about 1938, I think, when me dad took bad and he died quick. That left me mother in charge, because I were only 16." The story of Colin Marriott's life at Woodthorpe Grange is told later in this book.

Barbon Ensign drawn by Ted Hellaby.

Two other contributors remember Woodthorpe Grange before Colin Marriott took it over in 1959. **Grace Else** spent her young life there when her father, Ernest Smith, farmed it and **Henry Holmes**, brother to Mrs Ethel Hole, worked there for Ernest Smith when he was a young lad.

John Heathcote was born at Brassington. When he was about ten years old the family moved to Cromford. "They had a bit of a smallholding down there, but it never satisfied me, that didn't. I'd always got to be up at Gladwin Mark with me Grandfather and me uncles, because it were close on 300 acres, there were a lot more to do, cattle and horses and everything. After me grandfather died, the man that I worked for, he'd got two farms. He lived at the one down at Farley and I looked after Moor Farm for him for 14 years. But farm wages weren't good at that time, there were three children growing up. They didn't want to be miles from anywhere and you needed a lot more money so, in my late forties, I packed it up. We went to Cromford, but it weren't like living on a farm –

living on side of the road where folks were walking over doorstep more or less. It weren't a life as I were very fond on. Farming, it were a fantastic life, if I had opportunity, I could do it all again, I could."

Arthur and Mavis Hind both came from farming backgrounds. Mr Hind was born at Top Slack Farm where his father was the tenant farmer. Moving first to Goss Hall, then to High Ashes Farm, the family returned to Top Slack after the second world war. As a boy, Arthur began helping his father with the farm work. He has, together with his wife, farmed all his life. Though in his eighties he still does a little work on the farm and until recently had a milk round.

Olive Scott, (née Birks) also had farming connections with Slack Hill. "Grandfather's last posting was at Clay Cross and then he

bought the farm on Stonerows at Ashover. And that's where they were for, oh a good many years and then eventually they bought the one at the bottom of Slack Hill. And that's where he met his death, he were a bit impatient, instead of waiting for someone to help him he were trying to get what we used to call the shelvings on his hay cart and he had a rupture." Her father grew up on the Birks' farm at Knotcross and worked as a farm labourer. Olive herself, as a young woman, helped out at busy times, hay making and threshing and occasionally worked on a dairy farm at Ault Hucknall.

Olive's father as a young man.

Miss Lennox was the first woman to work for the Milk Marketing Board as a milk recorder. She visited designated farms to weigh the milk. She provides beautifully detailed cameos of some of the farms and their surroundings.

Clarice Hayes, née Robinson, was the daughter of the miller at Brockhurst. When she married she moved to Dicklant, Milltown. Her memories were recorded in the 1980s.

A number of contributors come from the hamlet of Milltown, Ashover, including life-long inhabitant, **Geoff Hammond**, a retired coach builder and **Lucy Moore**, whose memories of her Milltown childhood go back to the early 1900s. **Barbara Bark** (née Rickers) grew up there, she lived on Hockley Lane. **Tom Limb** was born and raised there. He still vividly remembers all the local small farmers of his youth. **Walter Hopkinson** was for many years the Milltown Postmaster and shop keeper. He was a keen gardener and helped out at busy times on the local farms. **Joe Holmes** also lived in Milltown for many years before moving to Ashover. He worked on a farm there during the difficult times of the 1930s. His father in law kept pigs and Joe helped look after them.

And finally, **Howard Davison**, whose richly detailed account of his farming life forms the backbone of this story, still farms at Dale Bank Farm, Milltown near Ashover.

Howard's parents both came from farming families. His mother's parents farmed at Milltown Farm.

"They were living there when she met my father and got married. Me father's parents farmed at Tupton and they were only on a rented farm. Eventually it came up for sale, but they

couldn't afford to buy it so they had to pack up farming then. And for a while me father worked for Clay Cross Council till he got married to me mother and he got this rented farm in Milltown at Demonsdale. Then his parents bought where I live now, and they moved there; and me father paid his parents so much a year to farm there. And when his parents died, the farm came to us then. That's how we ended up.

But he was in a bit better way then me mother. His father used to play in a dance band in his younger days and he used to have a squeeze box, a little melodeon, and they used to say, he'd be coming home at two o'clock in the morning with his dancing shoes and his squeeze box tucked under his arm. So, he had quite a nice younger life going to dances. I suppose that's where I've picked up my interest in playing the piano.

And of course, the welding side comes from me mother's father. He was very fond of blacksmithing. Wherever he farmed, he always built himself a blacksmith's shop and hearth and in his spare time he was knocking pieces of iron about. So when he moved onto Brown Lane he built himself a blacksmith's shop. He was a very handy stone mason as well, he had worked in Robin Quarry in his younger days. And that was the reason he died young, – he was only 64. He got pneumonia and it killed him. He'd got the stone dust on his chest and he couldn't get rid of it. So it was a short life for him really. I can see his blacksmith's shop now, a little shed on the end of a cowshed building and his hearth in it and an anvil. And me mother used to play about in that a bit as well. She'd get the fire going and warm bits of iron up and hammer them out and bend things in it. She was a bit interested in that as well. Aye. She'd quite a few talents if she could only have developed them."

Howard was born at Demonsdale Farm in 1925 and when he was two years old the family moved to Dale Bank Farm at Milltown where he still lives and works.

"During the early 1930's it was a very bad time for farmers. They'd a job to survive and it was a case of getting as much as you could and spending as little as you could, just to carry on. We milked about 12 or 13 cows, all hand-milked of course. We struggled on through the 1930's, I can't remember much about that because I was so young but I know we farmed with a couple of horses at that time. And it went on like that till the beginning of the war.

When war broke out things changed quite dramatically because there was a big demand for food. We started with a tractor then, with all the implements to it, and we got on a lot faster and produced more stuff. The pace of farming accelerated very quick then, once machinery came out. And of course contracting came into being then. Everybody'd got to plough up and grow corn and food and we got involved in that job in a big way. I was only 14 when war broke out and of course I couldn't drive on the road with a tractor. So he'd take the tractor and machinery and I should perhaps follow on, on me bicycle, and take over in the field. And that's how we carried on for a while, till I was 17, and I got my driving licence and then I was away. I was practically living on the tractor then, day in and day out, contracting, ploughing, discing, drilling, and corn cutting for everybody. We bought a binder in 1940 and we should be cutting about 120 acres a year with this binder. We'd our own farm work to do besides. In 1957 I bought a bigger tractor, second-hand. That made the job a bit easier.

Then, in the middle 50's combines started up here and I fancied the idea of a combine. In '59 I bought a little one and I was out contracting with that and I got more work and it got too much for the little combine, so I bought a bigger one in 1962. I also bought a brand new baler then and I was contracting and baling all the time as well as doing our own work at home. That combine lasted me until about 1970 and then I had another one, a bit better one and I still did quite a lot of hay-baling as well. Combining has gradually subsided as the years have gone on and as I've got older I've not managed to do so much work. When my father died that put a stop to a lot of things because I had enough on to work farming at home and the contracting side gradually ran down till I finished it off altogether.

The farm is 60 acres now. I think, when me father bought it in 1927, it was only 37 acres. He kept adding bits to it if there was a bit of land came available. And then, me mother's parents, they had a little farm in Milltown and when they died he inherited that land as well. And me mother had an uncle who died, on Ashover Hay, and he'd a few fields up there that we came into then. And that's what made our 60 acres now. It was quite big compared with some local farms in days gone by. It was quite a real viable farm. Because our stock totalled perhaps between 35 and 40 altogether. We'd have a dozen or more milk cows, and then there'd be all the calves. I think the most we ever had was 42 and we were just a bit too cramped up then. Previously we had two working horses. The stable they occupied, later on, we put cattle in there. And we used to keep pigs as well, they occupied another shed. As time went on, we didn't have pigs, and we didn't have horses, so there was more room for me father to house his cattle."

A FARMER'S CHILD

"I used to be on my knees –
I can't imagine how I singled all these swedes."

A child born into a farming family would start working as soon as he or she was able to do anything. Howard Davison soon found out that work came before play. Even a Christmas present might be an introduction to work: when he was six Father Christmas gave him a wheelbarrow.

TUPTON.
Nr. CHESTERFIELD.
To December 31 1931.

M+ B. E. Davison

In Account with G. T. Robinson,
WHEELWRIGHT & UNDERTAKER.
FUNERALS COMPLETELY FURNISHED.

£ s. d.

July 6th 1931 3 dozen iron washers : 9
1 New ladder 14 staves + 3 iron bolts
to same & painting £.18.6
November 3rd 1 new wood axle barrow
trundle + a new iron tyre to same . 9"0
& hooping + 1 nog to sole for wheel & painted . 3
December 5th 1 new milking stool . 2.6
1 new wheelbarrow complete
painted ---- for boy . 12.6

Total £ 2. 3. 6
2. 3. 6

Paid Feb 9

"And then, even later on, when I was going to Tupton Grammar School I should still have time to play sometimes at nights – lads'd come to play with me from school. But very often at certain times of the year, we should have to single two rows of turnips before we could play."

Miss Lennox once discovered two children who did have time to play.

"I went to a farm one early evening and there were two little girls in the yard. They'd got some canes in their hands, I said, "Are you playing at shop?" "No." they said, scornfully. I asked them some more questions and they looked at me as much as to say, "Silly old thing." In the end, I said – oh – they were in their dressing gowns, – "Are you going to bed then?" "No." I said," "Well what <u>are</u> you doing?" They said, "We're A.I. Men."

"You had a certain amount of play time but really it was hard work." says Millie Ablett.

"My job seemed to be weeding the yard from one end to the other. There was quite a stretch, and of course hay seeds – there were always something there. And we had hens, so we'd the job of collecting eggs and seeing if there were any gone broody, so we could put some under to have chickens. That was quite a delight if we could have some chickens."

Children on dairy farms learned to milk when young. John Heathcote learned on his grandfather's farm at Brassington.

"I were about seven year old and I learned to milk with a stone, jam jar and one hand. But I soon learned to milk properly with bucket and stool and that. Yes, best job, finest thing I ever learnt, farming. Nearly broke me heart when I packed it up."

Margaret Graney helped her father, Ted Hellaby, milk while she was still a school girl. He got up at 4.30 a.m. to get his cows milked and the milk to Stretton station by 7.00 a.m. Margaret would bring the cows up from where they were grazing, when she was not as tall as a cow's back. There would be 30 of them. Margaret herself would milk five at night, sitting on a three-legged stool, with one leg stretched out in case a cow kicked and with her head pushed against the cow's side. (If lice from the cow jumped onto you they died immediately, they couldn't live on humans.) At the weekends or during the school holidays she would milk ten.

Margaret would also take the horses to Hopkinson, the smith, to be shod. One was a Suffolk Punch and another had some thoroughbred to him. The smith must have preferred working with them to dealing with Margaret's donkey, who, while having her hooves pared would become so agitated that she would be climbing on his back as he persevered with the job. The cart horses had varied work.

"If they had dragged a huge load up from Stubben Edge, they would turn in at the farm gate and go straight for a drink at a huge trough. A team of them had brought this trough from Robin Hood Quarry. It was round, with no base, so a concrete base was made for it and it was set up in the yard. The horses knew to make for it."

Then, "as we got older," says Millie Ablett "we started helping on the farm properly."

As the farm work became more of a duty there was less time for leisure. John Heathcote describes how much commitment was needed.

"We used to go out, happen Saturday and Sunday nights. You didn't get a lot of time off though. It weren't same as it is now. You start at such a time and you're gone at such a time. You didn't knock off till work were finished. Didn't matter what day it were, whether it were Saturday or Sunday, you were still expected to carry on till it were finished. No saying "I've got to be at so and so at such a time." That didn't happen. If you were working properly, you worked as though it were your own."

If possible, it was perhaps as well to choose the job you did. As Millie explains

"I never did learn to milk, fortunately. If you once started a job you'd got it for life. I used to suckle the calves. You took the bucket with so much milk in for them. Some would suckle right away and another, you'd have to put your hand in the bucket and let it suck your fingers, then you gradually put it down into the bucket to start it to suckle. That would be for a time or two – then it got so it sucked itself. I liked that job. They nipped your figures at bit at times but that was a nice and rewarding job; you could see them growing."

Another of her jobs was delivering the milk.

"I used to take milk round. It was in individual cans, pint cans and quart cans and four pint cans. I used to have four or five in each hand. I used to have one or two "depots" where I used to leave them to ease the load, so I didn't have to keep going back home to refill the tins. I used to have four pints in the big one and then start pouring them out, (I could guess them to a fraction – how much a pint was in those days,) I did all Littlemoor, up Alton Lane, down as far as Dear Leap and down to bottom of Stubben Edge. I used to go down to the bottom of Stubben Edge on my bike, with a four-pint can on the handlebars. My brakes gave way one day and I finished up in Stubben Edge entry! I did that for several years, twice a day. Then we decided we'd leave night and just have it in morning. And then if I wanted to go out (I'd started courting) I'd have to find somebody to do the milk round). I was about 14, perhaps younger, when I began delivering the milk. I used to go down to Wilkinson's and one of the girls used wait for me going because she wouldn't let anybody else do her hair, only me. She'd a mass of curly hair. So I used to have to stop and do her hair. And perhaps go to shop for somebody else. You just did errands. And then my dad would say, "Oh, it'll soon be dinner time milk". (If you'd dillied and dallied a bit too long). In the winter, you just wrapped yourself up and got your boots on, and the gloves."

Mavis Brailsford too, before she was married, used to deliver milk to Overton on a bicycle. They had some wooden carriers made and they were fitted across the back of the bicycle. Besides those she had two crates of milk on the handlebars. With a full load the bike was unrideable; it had to be pushed. One icy winter, going along Gin Lane, the bike tipped over. There were broken bottles and milk everywhere! It was very hard work.

Her father, Alan Hodgson, knew George Kenning's secretary and

Mr Kenning said to him "I've got two cars." (They were American Willis Jeeps.) One was for Doctor Fine and the Hodgsons were pleased to buy the other one. Mavis now had four wheels! – even though the Jeep had a bullet hole in it. She had had driving lessons at Kennings and with old Mr Dimbleby, who ran one of the Ashover bus services. She took her test with milk bottles rattling about in the back. She hadn't had time to take them out.

There were seasonal jobs too. Mavis
> "used to help to turnip – pull, mangold – pull and pick potatoes. It was not very warm work and a back-aching job."

As a girl Dorothy Ward would work in the milking parlour. They had between 30 and 35 cows. They would not all be milked all the time. Some would be dry, because they were with calf.
> "You had two buckets of clean water because you had to wash the cows' udders before you started milking. We sang as we milked – hymns or songs like "Polly-wolly-doodle" or "Land of our Fathers". The cattle seemed to quite enjoy it." But, if it was a slow tune, we would hear, from the other end of the shed, Father calling "Come on then, let's change the tune." And uncle James would come in and say "Hey, you lot, less singing and more milking."

Only a croft separated their buildings from those of the next farm. At this farm there lived staunch Methodists. (Dorothy's family went to the Church of England in Lea where first her father and then Dorothy and her sisters and brother as they grew into their teens, became members of the choir and where Dorothy was Sunday School teacher.) After they had left Lea, their former neighbour missed them, saying there was "no singing, no singing at all."

   Dorothy also had the responsibility for caring for the working horses, for example driving the horse rake during hay-making.
> "Then, when a horse had finished work you had to take his harness off and, where he had been sweating, you wiped him with a damp cloth to stop him getting sore."

Other young people, not belonging to the family of the farm, might

choose to help with the farm work. Young Violet Gascoyne found this enjoyable, apart from one potentially frightening episode.

"I used to help on Brailsford's farm at Alton, help them milk the cows, help in the field. He taught me how you should milk the cows, I didn't actually milk but I learnt how to drive the tractor. We had lovely summer nights. Mrs Brailsford died and my mum was like a second mum to them. She used to go and wash for them and clean the house. We used to get our milk from the farm and mum used to ladle the milk out. People used to take a little can, like the lantern you carried with a candle in.

They let me drive the tractor, and one day my brother was on the top of the load of hay and I put the tractor out of gear and nearly threw him off the top. I was only about 12. Sometimes if they were desperate, I would have a day off school to help them. I used to be on my knees – I can't imagine how I singled all these swedes. It was just something you could do, and potato picking in the holidays."

Hilda Hopkinson also did this.

"If we wanted a bit of money I'd go with Bessie singling turnips. They had Northedge Fields. We'd walk across there, get down on our hands and knees and start singling these turnips. The rows were a mile long and we got two or three pennies a row. We took sack bags to kneel on and there we were, creeping up these rows."

A more enjoyable job, Howard Davison found, was to run errands to Billy Francis, the Littlemoor tinsmith.

"He was a general mender of everything for folks, a very clever chap. During World War II he was on secret government work with his tin-smithing, making something for the armaments. His father had a business before him. He also ran a lorry taking milk into the dairy. We had the 17 gallon churns and Billy and his father designed a locking device for the lid (so people couldn't help themselves to milk). We had a key and the dairy had a key.

I used to enjoy going up there and watching him at work, I should be about 12 years old. We'd take something and he'd mend it while we waited. He had soldering tools and special machines for rolling metal round and shaping it. He'd a little

Dec 2nd. 1933

Mr B Davison

Bought of *W. Francis*

Milk	12	0
Churn Lid	4	6
Patent Lid	1	0
	17	6

Paid

W. Francis

TELEGRAPH—"URTON LTD., CHESTERFIELD."
TELEPHONE No. 2854
NLA1.v.Bl. SHOWROOMS: QUEEN'S PARK ROAD

DIRECTORS:
W. H. URTON
E. L. URTON

West Bars,
Chesterfield,————— *Sept. 30* 193 8.

Mr B. Davison, Dale Bank, Ashover,

In Account with WILLIAM URTON, Ltd.,
IRONMONGERS, AGRICULTURAL ENGINEERS.

1938

June 15	Lift on Gun & Rifle 2/6			.	2	6
Sept. 15.	1 doz 1 Pt. Bottles 4.	1 doz ½ Pt. Bottles 3.		.	4	0
	1- Tube Caps 8d	1- Hose Union 1/2.		.	1	10
	1- Bottle Carrier 4/6			.	4	6
				.	15	10
Aug 3.	½ cwt Bdr Twine			1	1	0
				1	16	10

3237
Chesterfield, *12/10/* 193 8
Received for WILLIAM URTON, Ltd.,
the sum of *One* Pounds
Sixteen Shillings and *Ten*
Pence.
Urton
£1 :16:10

coke fire on his bench that he used to put his soldering irons
in and a little blow-lamp fired with methylated spirits, for
heavier soldering jobs and he used to make his own
electricity. He'd got a gas engine driving a generator for his
electricity that worked off town gas (not petrol) from the Clay
Cross Company. He was very ingenious. He used to make lots
of dairy equipment – siles, pint pots, half-pint measures,
quart measures, buckets, anything like that – even a cowl for
a chimney. When Bill died everything vanished, because his
son wasn't interested. Then of course, I took over and I
started mending for folks."

As he grew older, Howard appreciated visits to William Urton's
shop in Chesterfield.
"The big pot-bellied stove which stood in the middle of their
floor was stoked up till it glowed red-hot. The big counter was
all worn and scarred, and there were wooden shelves and
drawers. They'd have nuts, bolts, washers, candles, mantles
for gas lamps, nails, hammers, chisels – everything. They had
huge workshops in those days and a blacksmith's shop round
at the back of the main shop."

There were leisure hours. Millie Ablett remembers:
"Daddy Richmond, (the lengthsman) used to come into our
barn to eat his sandwiches and he always used to give us children a piece of white mint rock."

He would, too, repeat a rhyme which was a favourite with the children.

> We hope and trust and watch and pray
> For some fine weather from today
> So that the farmers can gather their hay

John Heathcote describes the way his children spent their leisure
hours and the simple pleasures they enjoyed.
"Sunday afternoons, in decent weather, when dinner pots
were washed up, we'd all go across fields and across a piece of
moor between Moor Farm and Bumper Castle. And down in
bottom, towards Burley Fields, there were an old nursery

where they used to grow heathers. And there were some beautiful heather and always some rhododendrons in flower, nearly all year round in this piece of nursery. Its gone now, they've ripped it all out and planted it up with pine trees. There were white rhodies, every time of year there were some rhodies, always some out. And we used to have a walk down there, and we'd got two or three goldfish and the children would be looking on ground, tipping stones over, collecting ant eggs from under stones, and taking 'em back and we enjoyed it. I can remember going down one Sunday afternoon, all of us. In this nursery there was a cabin and it had got stable doors on. Bottom part were shut and top part were wide open and one of 'em went towards this here cabin, and all of a sudden there were this owl, it were biggest.... massive owl, and it came through this open top door, and just over kids' heads."

There was pleasure too, for even the youngest child, in the work of milking.

"My earliest memories are from when I'd be about three or four years old, in the milking parlour with my parents hand milking. Dad would say "Come a bit nearer, come on, see where the milk's coming from." I'd edge a bit closer, Dad would turn the teat – milk would squirt into my face! Later on you learned how to turn the teat yourself and direct the milk straight into your open mouth."

Another worker who was not of employable age was Stuart Hole. When Mr and Mrs Fred Hole were the tenants of Lea Hall Farm, a travelling salesman came one day. As they stood at the farmhouse door talking to him he suddenly said "Look!" Their son, Stuart, who was about four years old, was standing under a cow. He was "milking" her by pulling at her teats. Fortunately he had chosen a placid cow, called Shirley, who was a favourite with him.

FARM WORKERS

"Everything was done by the horse:
hay-making, carting, ploughing, turnip pulling."

If children of the farm were expected to work, farm work was one of the few jobs available for country lads. These were the lowliest of farm workers. Olive Scott remembers being told about her father's unfavourable beginnings in farming.

"There used to be a pump down where the Red Lion is in the village here. And on the day that the farmers paid the rent up, they would go beering at the Black Swan then come and do their hiring. All the youths and lads who were wanting

The Birks family at Knotcross.
John Birks, seated, and his wife, Hannah front right.

work or hire got there. They used to go down and choose one they thought was suitable and my Dad was one that was picked, (him and another one,) and they went to a farmer at Dethick, – Lea way. They were pledged to go either six months or a year and they had to stick it whether or not. And I remember him saying that these two, – they didn't go inside – they used to have to sleep up in the barn among the hay. He wasn't very old, he'd be about 11 or 12, something like that. He'd a cat that he called his own at Knotcross. And I think he took it with him to keep him company and the little thing walked back from Lea to Knotcross again. It walked all that way! When his time were up he went back home and he worked on farm there."

Farms were worked by all the family members. At Sycamore Farm Millie Ablett's brothers

"worked with the horses. The younger of the two went to Eastwood Farm and Bill went up to Ravensnest to work for a while. And then, as my dad got older, both of them worked at home."

Extra help was always useful. Olive Scott helped with the work on a dairy farm:

"I used to help on a farm, it's right against Ault Hucknall Church. The people that went to this farm there, used to live up Butterley. Me sister worked there you see, in farm house and everything, she went with them when they moved. And then when they were very busy, harvest time or whatever, occasionally if I were at a loose end I'd go and help 'em. Collecting eggs, washing 'em and doing all sorts of jobs. It was better than my jobs in service, but I can remember, even there, it were hard work really."

There were always people who were pleased to help, for a consideration, as Miss Lennox remembers.

"Mrs Wells farmed at Rowsley. Six men who had to be at work at the Railway sidings at 7 o'clock, used to come to her at 6 o'clock and milk – they had their own stools in the cowshed, with their names on. In return, they had free milk."

During the second world war, when quarrying was in recession and working hours were curtailed, the workers might – as Joe Holmes did – make up the working week by doing farm labouring. For a miner the fresh air and exercise entailed in farming were a welcome change at the end of his shift. They were welcome because, as Miss Lennox explains:

"Farming was not a reserved occupation towards the end of the war – one farm I went to had ten men and they ended up with myself, two land girls and an old man who'd got one eye doing the lot."

Tom Limb's account of the daily work on a very small farm appears, on the surface, quite leisurely. It was, though, unceasing work.

"I remember Mrs Marsden saying one day – it was a cold, wet November day – "What have you been doing with yourself today, Mr Goodall?"

He says, "Like every other day. We get up in the morning at six o'clock, our Dick and me, we has a wash and a shave, we have eggs and bacon for breakfast, we sit listening to wireless – news – then we go outside, t'farm, (they only farmed in a very small way). 'Er (that's his sister) is us house-keeper'. He says "we milk, (they'd got one cow and a lot of young beasts) then we muck the cows out". What he didn't say was that for years and years and years, when I was a little boy, right up till they died – George used to come out with a wheelbarrow to the field at side, he'd go up a plank and shoot out the muck, and they'd a manure heap about 30 feet long and about eight feet high – ever so wide.

I should think it must have been there for about 40 or 50 years and, when the last one died in 1950 and they sold the farm, one of these horticultural suppliers that sold rotted manure bought the whole lot and when they cut into the old stuff it was just like dark flake tobacco. It was wonderful."

The Goodalls owned their farm but tenant farmers, as Arthur Hind explains, when their tenancy ended, had to "square up the manure heap." This meant first making it a yard high, then forming it into a tidy rectangle... The agent then measured it up to ensure that the outgoing tenant had left a good supply of nutrient for the fields.

But to go back to Mr Goodall:

"And then," he says, "we'd feed hens, potter about, then it'd be dinner time, (mid-day were dinner time) and that of ours'd have a dinner for us. We'd sit there till two o'clock, Dick and me. I'd be reading paper, our Dick'd be asleep (mind you, they'd be approaching 70) "come three o'clock we have to feed hens again". Mrs Marsden says: "Do you do that every day?" "Eeh aye," he says. "We've done it for 30 years. Nothing changes at our spot tha knows."

There were others though who worked full time. As Millie Ablett says

"Everything was done by the horse: hay-making, carting, ploughing, turnip pulling."

John Heathcote's early farming memories were all of horses.

"In the early days with me grandfather it were all horses. No tractors come to Gladwin Mark at all till war started. He loved his horses. Used to breed quite a lot. On a regular basis there'd always be four work horses, then some with foals. Most years we should have a couple of foals and young horses. Bring 'em on, break 'em in, get 'em used to work and then sell 'em. Some we kept, if they wanted replacing. If me uncles were wanting one they had some, if there were a good young 'un."

For Millie Ablett at Littlemoor too:

"We had working horses. It was all horse work. We had two, because you had one in the shafts and then a sling-gear horse, (the one in the front that was attached if you'd got an extra heavy load.) Some of the horses were all right and some wouldn't do as they were told and some wanted to come home before they'd done their work. If you'd just got the one it would get used to your voice and it would stop and start when you wanted it to. My brothers worked with the horses."

In the summer time the horses would be troubled by the swarming flies.

"I remember seeing the horses working with elderberry leaves tucked into their blinkers."

Decorating the horses in this way was meant to ward off the flies. The horses though actually made work, as she remembers.

"The horses had to be brushed down when they'd finished working because they'd be sweating. And you'd want a bucket or two of water. You had to carry the water to them. Clean them out by hand."

And John Heathcote explains that sometimes they caused even more work by their habits.

"Horses, work horses, they'd got a bad habit of backing up to a wall and pushing their behind on it and rubbing and rubbing. That used to fetch a lot of walls down. I remember my father in law, he had one and it were a terror for that. It did fetch some walls down, that did. I think it were because it had got itchy legs. They would be rubbing their legs, rubbing their behind. Horses tend to be a bit like that on their legs."

Another working member of the farm community was the farm dog. John continues:

"We always had dogs. We always had collies for cattle and everything. One of me uncles, he could train dogs for that sort of thing. He could train 'em perfect. We always had one, and usually two, really good dogs. Whenever it came to driving beasts or fetching beasts a good dog's worth half a dozen men. And we used to do a lot of driving, because we'd some ground at Stretton, and we used to drive beasts from Gladwin Mark to land at Stretton. Take 'em on road and drive 'em and put 'em in fields over there and leave 'em. And later on in the year you went and fetched 'em back. It would take all day but the dogs were marvellous. Couldn't have done it without the dogs. They'd know every road end and every gateway and which way to turn and they'd be up ahead to get 'em onto right road."

WOMEN AND HOME

"I can see the old pancheon in front of the fire,
with the bread rising. It's a lovely smell when it's baking."

Perhaps among the hardest workers were farmers' wives. Miss Lennox, who worked for the Milk Marketing Board remembers a farmer's wife:

"She was in her mid-twenties, two children, one in a pram and one about three. And they had to get the cattle in and have them ready for me to see. And she came running across when she saw my car. She said, "I haven't got them all in". It was such a small farm that the husband had to go and do jobs like hedging and walling to make ends meet. They milked these cows in the morning before he went and at night when he came back. And she would have to get them in. "But" she says, "I have to take the children with me, to get the cattle in and it's quite a job getting a pram over a ploughed field.""

Besides helping with the farm work, and providing extra food at hay making and harvest times, the wives and mothers had all the washing and cooking of the household to do. Howard's mother

"Did all her own washing in the copper. Aye, she'd stoke that up in a morning and boil all the clothes in that. And the dolly pegs and the old wooden mangle, of course."

This work might be done in conditions that were not particularly helpful. John Heathcote explains that at Moor Farm

"All the water that you used were pumped. There was no electric. No gas. I remember when we first went there, the man that I worked for, they'd lived up there and they'd had Calor gas and he says "There's a gas cylinder connected up and another spare un." And they were about 15 shilling apiece

these gas cylinders, then. Anyway I paid him. I don't know
whether we paid him for one as was connected, I know I paid
for the other and for one light, just the one light in kitchen,
altogether, that were £3. summat and they lasted about five
weeks between 'em. And so that were end of them, we didn't
bother wi' them no more. Couldn't afford to. And actually, for
knocking about in yard, we had pressure lamps. Paraffin
lamps, that you pumped up and they were a marvellous light,
but when you get them at side of electric light they weren't
much good at all."

Miss Lennox relates an incident which testifies to the lack of
amenities even on good farms:
    "The other side of Chatsworth Park they had a very big farm;
    Chatsworth did, with a milking parlour and everything. I
    remember one morning – and it seemed bitterly cold in those
    winters – the herdsman was milking. The house that they
    had on the farm would be a couple of hundred yards from the
    milking parlour. And they were always told, (not by me), to
    bring me a tray of tea when I got there in the morning. And I
    can see now this man doing things and I was with my charts.
    And he used to call me "Miss" – he said, "What time do you
    make it, Miss?" I said, "Quarter past six". It was snowing
    hard. And all of a sudden a little woman came, covered in
    snow, with a tray. She'd walked – with the teapot and all the
    things for my tea – in this. And he greeted her with – he
    looked at his watch, he said, "Do you know, it's twenty past
    six". He said, "Some people would stay in bed all day,
    wouldn't they?" And she said, "Oh yes, I'm ever so sorry. I
    couldn't get the fire to go, to boil the kettle". No conveniences!
    They don't know they're born these days. I think of these
    things when people are grumbling."

Nell, John Heathcote's wife, cooked with a coal fire.
    "There were a beautiful range in, only it were coal. We
    managed all right, course we did. I mean we'd been brought
    up to that sort of a life: paraffin lamps, and everything else.
    That were first thing me mother used to do in a morning after
    she'd had breakfast, go round wi' paraffin and check lamps,
    and get 'em ready for lighting at night. Washing was in what

we called washhouse, outside where pump were. There was a big copper in corner and when it come to washday, get a big fire going under that and boil that and put clothes in. In early days it were dolly pegs and then we got a ponch."

Howard's mother
"Had a range with a side oven, a side boiler and the old fire in the middle. And then a great big chimney up above. She did all her cooking on that. She'd bake bread. Ah, she'd happen do eight or nine loaves, something like that. She had flour delivered from Woodheads at Chesterfield. They delivered every month and there'd be no end of bags of flour come and all other sorts of things as well. The bags of flour I should think they'd be a stone. You know, 14 pounds, stone bag – brown paper bag. I can see 'em now. Yes. And I can see the old pancheon in front of the fire, with the bread rising. It's a lovely smell when it's baking. Lovely to eat as well but it goes fast. There'd be me mother and father and me and very often a farm man as well. We should shift some bread. Because me father could eat. I know, I'd never a big appetite. She used to bake cakes as well. She was a very good cook. She used to do jams. We grew our own fruit. Ah, we'd always apples and plums. I don't think we ever had pears. We were never keen on pears. But I know we'd always apples and plums and raspberries, blackcurrants all that sort of fruit. There was nothing wasted. It all was made up into food. And of course, in the early days, we were pig killing as well. And she'd all the pork to cope with. And she made pork pies and there was all sorts of stuff.

Early on, she made butter. I can remember her making butter."
Mrs Ethel Hole describes how it was done.
"The warm milk was put into a large pancheon (a big earthenware bowl which was glazed inside.) This was kept on a cold stone in the pantry for about a week until there was enough to make several pounds of butter. The cream was stirred each day. The churns were mostly made of wood. I have a glass one that made a pound or two."

The Davisons' churn was earthenware.

"I think I've still got the earthenware churn, but the wooden bits have gone years ago. I can remember doing a bit of churning for her – it wasn't one of the end-over end churns though, it was a round earthenware churn. It had a long handle with a round piece of wood at the bottom of it with holes drilled in it. And you podged it up and down in the milk till it turned to butter. There was a big wooden lid, with a hole in the middle, where this shaft went through, fitted on top of the churn, to stop it splashing out, till it started to go into butter. And then she'd these butter pats as well, to shape it up and leave patterns on it. I think that was in the very early days, when I was a little kid, because gradually, as you could buy decent butter, home butter making stopped. She never did make cheese."

John Hodgsons' mother did.

"We used to source good milk from Ayrshire cows from dad's cousin. There'd been some misunderstanding one day, we got short of milk, we rang through and they said "you can get some from so and so" – and it's a black and white herd. They get it home and mother says "This is no good, it's not fit to sell." They had to use some of it for orders then mother says "I'll make cheese with the rest." She went and got the rennet and made cheese – mother – she could do anything. Do you know, this cheese was identical to Lancashire, it was brilliant."

Women also helped with the dairying. John Heathcote's wife,

"Nell, eh she did everything. She could milk cows but she didn't like doing it. When I were at Moor Farm I used to be milking ten, twelve beasts on me own, apart from doing the tractor work on both farms. Sometimes I might be a bit late going back home to start milking. Then, if the kids were in bed, six, seven o'clock, or if they had had their tea and they were settled she'd come and bring a bucket and while I were milking she'd bring me empty bucket and put it down in window in cowshed and I'd milk and I'd put me full one on't window and she'd come and empty it."

This work had been passed down from one generation to another.

"I had an aunt and she looked after, I should think there'd be three lads, husband and me uncle and the house. She were always working, like Nell. And when you got up in a morning she'd follow you downstairs straight away and then she'd come down into cowshed with a big jugful of tea and teacups and a piece of scone or summat like that for everybody, first thing in the morning. Then back in house, take pots back, and come back and bring bucket and stool and that and come and help you milk so many cows and then go back and get breakfast ready. I think women had a hard time really.

The only time Nell's mother went off o' t'farm was Saturday when she went on the bus to do shopping, in Chesterfield. Previous to that they had a pony and cart as they used to go shopping with. She used to take so many eggs and go to Chesterfield. I think they used to leave pony and cart at one of the public houses in Chesterfield. She'd have people that she took eggs to, that'd order them. She had to take eggs because that were part of shopping money when she got there. In them days eggs were about, well at most a shilling a dozen."

It was women's work to rear calves and this was Dorothy Ward's favourite job.

"To teach them to drink, you would first get a bucket of milk to the right temperature, then you would dip your fingers in and put them into the calf's mouth. Gradually you would be able to lower your hand into the bucket and the calf would be so busy sucking at your fingers that it would, unawares, be drinking from the bucket. Then it would accept the bucket happily."

Even when, later, Dorothy moved to Woolley farm she loved to rear the calves. As they grew older she would go down the drive to the field to fetch them in, calling "Mummy's babies." They didn't need to be driven, they would follow her into the shed. Her husband would chide her, wondering what people would think if they heard, but it made no difference. "They <u>are</u> my babies." she would answer.

It might have been an easier job than feeding the hens. Margaret Graney's mother's jobs were suckling the calves and feeding the fowls.

"I don't know if she fed them all – there were about three thousand. To feed the ones housed in the Orchard you had to go through a stile. A fierce cockerel would meet you there. Margaret's mother always went with a stout stick and every time she knocked him unconscious. Even when she told her husband, "He won't get up again," he always survived."

Howard's mother

"Always kept a lot of hens, I can't remember how many, there were no end in the stack yard. The eggs used to be sent to a packing station somewhere. They were collected every so often and my mother had to see they were all clean of course. They had to be washed, some of them, and put into these big crates ready for being picked up. That was another side line that we had. She used to sell no end of eggs. Ah, it was a hive of industry, our farm was in those days."

Eva Butler remembers her grandmother's

"chickens running about this field. She had them for years. She worked at the school canteen and when she came off the two

Brown Leghorns.

June 11th 1986.

Buff Leghorns.

o'clock bus, they let her take, in those days, (they wouldn't let you do it now,) a bucket and she'd bring the scraps. And the chickens would go on the road and meet my mother off the bus. They knew when she was coming and they'd go on that road and meet her and come back with her. And they'd all got pet names. One was called Mama's little baby."

And the work entailed
"Grandad growing corn in the back croft for Granny's hens. Reaping it himself with a scythe. I can see him now with his cap. He used to take his cap off and mop his brow. They fed the hens with that. I don't know if they dried it and just bashed it and swept it up. They'd perhaps throw it as bedding and the hens helped themselves to the grain."

"A DIY job, as you might say" adds Millie Ablett.

"Granny used to boil potatoes and make the mash and they used to have maize, to make the egg yolks yellow."

She remembers too the inevitable end of Granny's rabbits and chickens.

"In the war time, we reared rabbits and ate them. When meat was rationed and scarce. People used to say, "I don't know how you could". But we could. And we used to do boiling fowl. One that had finished laying. It was delicious. It had flavour, because it had run up and down the fields, picking up bits and bobs. And there were no foxes in those days, or very few."

The strong smell of tobacco pervaded some farmhouse homes, as Joe recalls.

"Oh the farmers were old fashioned up there. One chap used to smoke herbal tobacco in a pipe, it was just like following a bonfire around. You could smell him a mile off, herbal bacca. Ever so cheap it were, you could smell him a mile away with that damn stuff. I didn't go in the house when he'd got that going. It was bad enough outside."

At one time others would have had to endure such powerful aromas. Bert Hopkinson remembers that at Revel Farm

"When we were gardening or working in the turnip field we were used to seeing clay pipe stems. Once I found a fine bowl, shaped like a man's head. We heard of farmers who smoked dried tea leaves, dried horse manure and clover leaves. But by the 1950s Woodbines were very popular, in paper packets at five for two pence and clay pipes fell out of use."

Millie Ablett describes how Sunday was observed.

"Sunday was a day of rest. You had your food, you went a walk. There was no playing football. No knitting, no sewing, no nothing. You didn't wind wool. You didn't do anything on a Sunday that could be classed as work, apart from the food. I remember my mother stitching a button on something. I remember her saying, "Well, it's black cotton. It'll not matter for today".

The cold weather could make life miserable.

"We hadn't the comfort that we have nowadays." says Howard. The cold would get right into the house. We'd no heating apart from an open fire in the living room, and the bedrooms, they were like ice-boxes. Because they weren't just cold, they'd be damp as well. I don't know how ever I used to survive in that bedroom. But evidently when we were young like that, we didn't feel the cold as bad. Couldn't have done. Eeh no, I couldn't sleep in that room now without some heat on it. Because I'd got the end bedroom, it was the coldest of the lot. The windows, there'd be solid ice on the inside in the morning, you couldn't see through them. All coated in ice, and it wouldn't be much better round the bed either. No, some things you wouldn't want to go back to.

I remember that 1947 winter. My father had pneumonia and I'd got the lot to do myself, with my mother. Oh. It was a terrible nightmare. We'd all our mangolds and turnips in those two fields against the Greyhound and we couldn't get them out of the fields, it was so wet. The prisoners of war helped us get that field off. They helped to pull all these turnips, a gang came every day and they pulled these mangold and turnips and cleaned them and chopped the tops off and we pitted them at the bottom of the field because we couldn't get out at the top, it was too wet. We shut them up and then covered them with straw and soil to keep them frost-free and, during that rotten bad winter, I was going down there with a horse and a sledge. We pulled the wall out at the bottom of that field against this pit and I was bringing mangolds and turnips home in bags to feed the cattle every-day. And my father lay in the house with pneumonia. That went on all that winter. I shall never forget that. It were a real rough do."

But generally the family was healthy.

"We got colds and perhaps occasional 'flu, anything like that. But we never seemed to ail much. Not as much as we do now. There were none of these modern diseases that we come across now. They weren't known in those days. There were only simple basic things and I think, with farming, we lived a healthier life as well. We weren't meeting up with diseases

anywhere. It was an outdoor life and we ate healthily and
lived healthily and that was as long way towards it. I do
remember once, I nearly got lock-jaw. Because, I was a little
kid, running about in the yard, and we'd a chap working for
us – he was mucking a cow-shed out and he came out of the
doorway with a shovel full of muck and the corner of the
shovel caught me on the side of the lip here. I didn't think
anything about it but suddenly I was taken quite ill and we
didn't know what was wrong with me. And me mother got in
touch with the doctor. We had an Alfreton doctor at that time.
I don't know how she did it, because we had to go down into
Milltown, to the quarry, to telephone. That was the only place
that had a telephone in those days. I should think she rang
the doctor up. He came out to me and he said, "you're on the
verge of lockjaw". And I don't know what he did, but he pulled
me round from it all right and I didn't have any after effects.

Ooh, and I had shingles as well. That was horrible. And
there were nothing they could do for me. We were corn-
cutting at the time and I'd got them all round me waist and
itchy – itchy, painful, rotten things they were. And I
remember I'd no shirt on. I left me shirt off when we were
corn-cutting. I was driving the tractor and we were bindering
at the time. And I remember just sitting on the tractor and
keeping me back from touching anything. And oh! it was
agony in bed at night, on these nasty itchy spots. And I
remember, I felt them for two years, before it finally
disappeared. Things like that just stick in me mind. But
they're about the only things that ever I caught."

THERE WERE LITTLE FARMS
ALL OVER

*"A lovely summer morning, the sun shining and old Harry Robinson,
he'd be in one of his fields, swinging his scythe, mowing his grass
and singing at the top of his voice."*

There were many very small farms in this part of Derbyshire.
John Heathcote's father in law, in the 1930s, farmed about 25
acres.
   "He never kept milk cows, just one, happen, to feed a calf or
   two, and for their own use; but they never sold any milk or
   anything like that. He used to rear calves and sell them when
   they were stronger. They'd hens and all sorts, he had that.
   Pigs, he used to fatten pigs up and sell 'em. Rear pigs."

Sometimes it was possible to acquire more land, to add to the farm.
   "He bought a bit more....Originally his farm – you went down
   a lane and the wall was the boundary of their farm. And
   eventually he bought the ground on the other side of the wall.
   He bought all ground, didn't buy farm and buildings. When he
   farmed it, it was ever such a nice, clean, tidy place."

Such a farm might not be economically viable.
   "That's why" says John, "he got his job on the council."

A man needed many skills because often farming was combined
with another occupation. The miller at Brockhurst combined
milling with farming as his daughter, Clarice Hayes describes.
   "He were a big lashing fellow. He could do anything, I think,
   my father could. He were really in demand – when there were
   cows calving, or if a cow or calf were wrong or anything like

that, people from round about'd fetch my father. On the hill above the mill, there was an old lady lived, and she'd three lads. And some of them'd come across and they'd say, "We've a cow due to calve today". And they were going to work, and "Would he be keeping an eye on 'em?" And he'd go across and look at this cow. And he'd think her'd be calving later. And Mrs Ward used to say, "I shall come on hill in the night and I shall hang a light on a tree". And we used to look for this light on tree, then he knew cow were shaping like having this calf, and he'd go across. That used to take place, generally at night. It was so funny; such a lot of their cows went wrong. They used to wonder in them times if it were where these cows went to drink."

Howard Davison's farm was quite large by local standards. On the smaller farms round about, the work, although it was similar, would, necessarily be done a little differently. Howard takes a tour round Milltown, Ashover, remembering all the little farms there once were.

"After me father died, and I was farming on my own, I remember that an old chap, who was at other side of Brackenfield, somehow found out I'd some hay to sell and he walked to my place to have a look at the hay. He went in under the hay barn and he kept pulling handfuls out and smelling at it, and he'd go to another place and pull a bit more out and smell at that and he decided eventually it <u>was</u> good hay and he'd have some. So I had to load it up and take it to 'em. We baled hay at that time, so I loaded it myself at home and took it to them and threw it off and these two chaps built it into a little heap at the side of the cowsheds. That was it. And the boss-man of the family, he came quietly to me and asked me how much it was. I told him and he disappeared for quite a while into the house, and then he came out and we went into a quiet corner somewhere and he counted all these pound notes out to me. It was all in cash. He paid me in cash. And he was that secretive about it all. Mustn't let anybody see it, aye. They were almost novelty people. They've eventually all died off now. They've gone. I think somebody's bought the house and farm buildings and they're doing it all up and I don't know what'll happen to it eventually. It'll never be the same again. No. No. It's another stage in farm life that's disappeared there. They lived 50 years previous to everybody else, in the real old-fashioned style. They didn't have horses even. There was a big family of them and they were very close-knit. I think there were four brothers altogether and there'd be three or four sisters as well. I think there was only one ever got married. All the rest just lived at home in this farm house. They were a most peculiar family but they were nice people.

They farmed in the by-gone days good and proper. They didn't have any plough ground at all. It was just grazing land and a little bit of hay. They mowed it all by the scythe and made it by hand, and carried it to the stack by hand. They had just a few cattle but I don't think they ever sold these cattle. They kept them till they eventually died of old age. They had to buy a bit of corn for the cattle feed. And the corn traveller (from Bailey's at Matlock) used to call, once a month or so, to take a little order for the corn. And they would have him in the house, to give him his order – and pay him of course, because that was most important. They never owed a penny to anybody. They'd almost pay you before they had the goods. They were very strict about that. But he used to tell us these little tales about these folks. They always wore clogs, these folks did, and they'd nothing on the floor in the house, only stone flags. And he'd knock on the door and he'd hear a clatter of these clogs on this stone floor and then one body'd come to the door and let him in and there'd be just that one body in the house, everything else had vanished. But there were gaps under the doors leading off from this room, where the stone flags had worn away. And he said, you could see a row of clogs under these doors. They were the old latches on these doors, where you put your finger through the hole, to lift the latch up. And at every hole, there was somebody's eye, looking through this hole! The occupants were all behind these doors, watching. But you could see the clogs under the door. And he said the table stood in the middle of the floor. And where the table legs stood, the stones were higher than all round it. The stone flags had worn away with these clogs and left the little bits of stone under the table legs standing higher up. It was a real novelty to go into that place. At the outside door, the step had worn so low the hens could go under. And he said sometimes, when he'd knocked, he could hear hens prating as this person shuffled through them coming to the door. Oh, it was worth visiting. And they lived to ever such a big age, these folks did, into their eighties and nineties. They lived ever so primitive and yet they must have been very healthy. They never had a doctor, no, they didn't. They seemed to survive without a doctor.

There was a little farm like that on Ashover Hay

"There were two brothers who farmed on the Hay. One of them had put sticks down this particular field, to make a straight line. The other brother carted a load of muck down into the field to pull it out in heaps, down the field. When he got there he looked down these sticks and they weren't in line. So he took his load of muck back home again and told his brother that these sticks weren't in line and he'd got to straighten 'em so that when he pulled out his heaps of muck they would be in a straight line.

There was a chap, Mr Gregory, lived near the top of the Hay during the War and he used to send one churn of milk. And the lorry that picked it up used to back down from the top of Knotcross Hill, right down to that farm and pick this one churn of milk up from the gateway. Before they widened it, the lane was ever so narrow. He used to have to back down so far and they dragged the churn up there on a little trolley, with the milk in it and left it to be picked up there. And I can see Mr and Mrs Gregory, dragging this trolley with the one ten gallon churn on, up that slope, to where the lorry could pick it up. And it'd be no easy job because it wasn't a nice trolley. Four small wheels on it, either iron or wooden, and Mr Gregory'd be dragging it up with a handle at the front and Mrs Gregory'd be pushing behind. It was a backbreaking job for them really. They'd got to get it out of the yard, to start with, and it's ever such a steep, cobbled yard. I don't know however they struggled up that yard with it every day, but they did. And eventually Council widened that road up there and the lorry came down to the yard end after that. Well, they thought it was marvellous then! They'd only just got to get it to the yard gate.

We used to mow for him, get his hay and little jobs like that, just to feed his few cows. And then, on Dicklant, Clarice Hayes lived there. Well, they used to make one churn of milk. I used to do all their mowing and they used to make the hay and then I used to bale it for them. And then there was Steven Hopkinson at the bottom of Dale Bank. They were another little farm. They did have a little tractor and do their own work. But they weren't in as big a way as we were. They had either one or two churns perhaps at most and the milk lorry picked theirs up.

Lower down the Hay, there was a chap called Joe Chamberlain. He had the bit of land over the back and then he'd all the buildings at West View. He had an old tractor and a few cows and he used to cultivate that land on the Stonerows Lane side, and I used to do odd little jobs for him as well. He had the odd cow or two and he used to go on there every morning, milk his cows and carry the milk back here in buckets. I used to see him tramping across those fields, with a bucket in either hand, bringing his milk back from his cows that he'd milked there. And then he'd have a calf or two that he'd suckle as well over there, with the milk that he didn't want at home.

Where the ruined cottage is, that was another farm, Harry Robinson lived there with his brother. They lived on Oakstedge Lane and had two fields there before they moved on to Hay Lane. They had these one or two cows and a calf or two. I think there was about nine or ten acres belonging it and I did a little bit of work for Harry. He'd a little plot just topside the old cottage, in the top of the field. He used to grow a few turnips and things on it for his cattle and I used to plough that for him. He used to mow all his hay with a scythe. And I can always remember, a lovely summer morning, the sun shining and old Harry Robinson, he'd be in one of his fields, swinging his scythe, mowing his grass and singing at the top of his voice. It was a pleasure to hear him. He'd mow his grass, then he'd turn it and shake it about by hand and he'd carry it all on his back into the stack yard and pile it up for his cattle. I know the field wasn't far from his house but he'd carry it on his back in forkfuls. He did that for years. And he'd also a paper round that chap had. He used to take a great bundle of papers all round everywhere on his push-bike. He'd this bundle of papers on the cross bar and he couldn't ride it because there were too many papers on, he'd push it round. Of course, he'd be able to ride it back when he got rid of his papers. But he'd be all round Littlemoor, Handley, Woolley, delivering these papers. I don't know whether he picked them up at Ashover. But he delivered these papers every day.

I used to go down with my father to Tom Willmot the blacksmith. I was fascinated, watching all the proceedings. He had a very gruff manner. As I got older, I used to enjoy going down and blowing fire up on the hearth, blowing the bellows. The bellows were made of leather, about three inch diameter, about four inches deep with a big long handle on the top. When you pulled the handle the bottom came up and down again. A spout came out from it into the hearth to blow the coal up. He didn't let me do anything else, that was the limit of my work – I suppose he'd let anybody blow up because it relieved him of a job. He had to blow the fire up all the time there was a piece of metal in the fire because it didn't retain the heat. As soon as you stopped blowing the coke'd go from bright red to dull red and gradually sink and sink and it'd almost go out. It'd got to have a draught all the time to keep it burning. It was a special type of coal or coke. If he was happen doing something else, happen bolting something together, his fire'd go black. There might be a faint glow right in the bottom. Then he'd have to start and blow again and it would gradually build up until it was almost a white heat again. Underneath the hearth there was a big stone trough full of water for quenching the metal off. The edges of the stone trough were worn away with sliding pieces of metal in and out. It dipped down in the middle ever so hollow. And the hearth itself – it was a stone hearth – had worn away in the middle. Whenever my father went down to the blacksmith, I should go with him, until I got older then I should go on my own. He was a busy man. He used to have a vegetable garden in a plot on Brown Lane. He'd some cowsheds at Fallgate and some cattle of his own. He'd happen have a cow for his own use. And he'd two fields up Gin Lane where he used to mow hay and then he'd a little field at the back of where he lived. He'd turn his cattle – he'd perhaps only have one cow, a calf

The two storey cowshed is clearly shown
in this old painting of The Greyhound, now The Nettle.

or two – into that field. He was doing this bit of farming
among the blacksmithing.

At the Greyhound, they'd do a bit of farming as well. Those
fields at the back belonged to the pub and the owner, he'd
have a few cows and milk a bit in among his publican's work.
A lot'd be like that in them days. There were cowsheds both
sides of the Greyhound but the cowshed where the post box is
was rented by another small farmer. This was a two storey
building with a chamber above and outside steps leading up
to it."

My grandfather farmed on Brown Lane. He had a few cows
he milked and he had a little milk round. Every day he used
to bring his milk all round this area. He'd have a big basket-
ful of little milk cans, pint cans. We used to do his work for
him, mowed his grass and got his hay for him, farmed his
little plot there. He'd only about ten acres I think. He had
come from Milltown Farm which he used to farm. There was

another little farm on Dark Lane. There was one at the top of Butterley and then there was the other farm below, coming down Butterley, that's always been a farm. And you come down the hill again to that bottom bungalow where my mother's uncle lived. He used to farm a bit there. He'd some buildings across the road from that bungalow and he had a cow or two and made a drop of milk and I've an idea he made cheese. There were little farms all over."

THE FARMING YEAR

"To everything there is a season...
....a time to plant and a time to pluck up that which is planted."

THE FARMING YEAR: PLOUGHING

There is an entry in Ted Hellaby's Diary for 31 December,

" And so comes the last."

Although this was the end of a year, for the farmer working arable land, the year does not begin and end, it is a continuous cycle. As soon as harvesting is finished ploughing begins, and continues into the new year, preparing the ground for seed sowing.

When Howard Davison's father ploughed with horses it was, usually, a peaceful scene.

"You could just hear a sliding noise as the furrow were turned, that's all. You know the sound that a spade makes when you push it into the soil – similar to that. It was very quiet – unless you hit some stone. And if you'd got what we called "ratchel," softish stone, close to the surface, it'd make a chattering sound as it ran over that. It was a quiet job, ploughing with horses."

It was a skilled job to guide the plough but if you had a trained team:

"A good pair of horses, they'd know what to do on their own. They knew the command, to turn either left or right when they came out at the end of a furrow. It was "ov" and "gee", one word meant turn right and the other meant they turned left. They didn't need to use the reins to turn 'em, they'd turn with this command. And of course they stopped when you said

Bernard Davison ploughing with a single furrow plough

"Whoa!".

A plough'll turn a furrow out and it could be perhaps ten inches wide in the bottom. It made a little track to walk in and it seemed to come natural to the horse to put one foot in front of the other. It'd be a nice, flat, solid bit to walk on. So, I suppose he'd feel it'd be better to walk on that than one foot on loose ploughing or on a step. The other horse'd be on top, outside, on the land that hadn't been ploughed. You could put a horse with big feet on that.

I remember my father ploughing with a couple of horses and his single furrow Ransome plough. He'd go and do his stint in the field after he'd done his yard work. He'd not have many hours a day to work in the fields ... he did employ a man, but even so they'd still all cattle to see to, so he'd just have a few hours in the middle of the day for his ploughing. But a ploughman who was working on a big farm would take his horses out first thing in the morning. He'd perhaps plough eight hours and he'd manage to plough an acre in the day if he went well. On these big farms they might have a dozen teams of horses and ploughmen. I've known big farms having as many as 24 horses on the farm and perhaps a dozen workers as well. And they'd all go out ploughing with teams of horses and they'd cover bigger acreages then, with having so many men to do it. But one man on his own, he'd have to work hard to plough an acre in a day. And in that time he'd walk 16 miles. So you were getting plenty of exercise."

The harness the horses wore was quite complicated.

"Ah well, you get the collar round their neck and then the hames, that's the metal strips round the collar that the chains fasten to, for whatever they're hauling. The head gear is called a bluft. That carries the bit in their mouth and also leather shields round the sides of their eyes, to stop them being scared by, perhaps, objects to the side of them which might frighten them. And then, across their back are the plough pads that support the chains going back to the plough. The chains on the plough are attached to swingel-trees that keep them proper width apart so that they don't rub on horses' back legs. And then they're anchored to the plough

The harness is clearly shown in this photograph of Ronnie with Beauty and Bess at Hilltop Farm Ashover. 1927.

and that's how they haul it along."

Olive's father could do all sorts of jobs on the farm, among them, ploughing:
"I've got a photograph of me Dad, he were ploughing in that field at bottom of Butterley and he's got one of these big horses and an ordinary plough. He were a good farmer, there were no doubt about that. I mean the times they went up and down a field with a plough and a horse. They'd got to sort of o' dig plough in, in a way."

With well trained horses, this job must have been satisfying. Lucy Moore remembers watching as a child:
"There was Richard Goodall doing his ploughing with a grey horse. It was war-time, first world war, and there was not much in the way of Christmas presents. We had been sent some gloves, knitted ones. And of course we, myself and my sister Dorothy, were eager to try them on. So mother said, "Well you'll have to go out". Well it wasn't many yards from West View, round the corner and up the hill to Richard Goodall's field. And I can always remember proudly wearing my new gloves, standing watching him through the gate, ploughing with a one-horse plough. His mother had been keeping her eye on Richard. She used to say, "However quiet your horse may be, never loose the rein."

Ploughing was a job which Miss Bassett found challenging.
"Of course, we used to use horses instead of tractors. And, well, I have just managed to use a plough but I wouldn't say I could plough. It was too much like hard work with a team of horses. But it was all in a day's work. From early morning."

Howard explains exactly how he sets about the job.
"When you plough, you usually start up the longest side of a field. You make what we call a headland mark all the way round about. I measure 15 feet out from the wall, and just scratch a little mark out with the plough, and you plough to this mark. You start off up the longest side or straightest side and so far in from the headland and you set what we call a rigg. (that is the first indentation.)

When you plough in stubble you open up the rigg by ploughing a single furrow. Then you go back the other way and open it, leaving a trench. When you've got that, you turn round and go back and turn that lot back again – you bury it the other way. Then you turn round and go back again and bury that one – turn that one again. So all that lot that's opened up gets buried – all the ground's been ploughed – its all been disturbed.

When you are ploughing in grass you go up the field with one very shallow furrow and two a little bit deeper. And you turn round at the end of the field and you come back. And you bury that little shallow furrow with another one turned on top of it so that there's a strip buried underneath the furrow that doesn't get ploughed. So it levels the whole lot up. And your other two furrows, with a three furrow plough, they gradually get to the full depth: with my ploughing, about five or six inches deep. I don't go any deeper than that because our land, it's stony and clay and all sorts, and you don't want that turning up on the top. So usually that's the depth I plough at.

Anyway, you go down, burying this first little furrow. And after that you start and plough the normal depth. Keep going round the rigg until you reach the headland mark at the side of the field. When that's done, go across the field, measure a certain distance across and set another rigg same as that first one. Plough round that and then, when you've done so much of that, there's another strip between that rigg and the first one still to plough. So you split that and work in till you've ploughed that in from either side to finish a furrow in the middle. And to finish the furrow, you have to keep it parallel both sides, so it comes in square. When it's getting, say ten or fifteen yards left to plough, I measure across with a measuring stick, and, if it is out anywhere, run narrow furrows off to square it up ready to finish, and then work in to the last little bit. With a three furrow plough, next to the last time up the field, the third furrow (the last one) is left very shallow. And you scheme it so that there are two furrows left to plough. That's the final run down. Then the run up is a very shallow furrow, last one. You turn round at the end of the field and come back. Your plough is bringing the two furrows, full furrows and the third plough is taking a little bit deeper out of that shallow bit that was left before, so you finish a furrow there, with that last furrow half turned over with the back plough share. And in my case, the idea is to leave it as shallow as possible so that it works down fairly level afterwards, so you've not got a deep furrow to work over for the rest of the time. Otherwise you can't finish a nice neat furrow and you get weed growing in it and all untidy everywhere, so it's most important to have both sides parallel to finish off.

It's not quite so important when we're drilling corn, but it's always better to keep a straight side and then everything seems to fit in better when you're finishing off. When you're drilling a field of corn you can plan it that you don't have a lot of unnecessary running about and not working. So it's just as well to plan your work out as you go along to minimise time wasted.

Ah, then the following year, you set the rigg in the furrow of the previous year and turn your soil the opposite way, so it keeps the land level all the time. And then of course, when you finish your field like that, you've just the headland to plough. And you start and go round the field until you've finished. One year you'll turn the furrows out of the hedge and the next year, you'll turn them into the hedge. So you keep the soil in its proper place all the time. And that's how my ploughing's gone on all me life."

Howard explains how he began ploughing:
"I started on tractors, because me father bought a tractor when I was 14. Previous to that I perhaps went in the field with him but I should play around and not take a lot of notice of it really. I never handled horses. I grew up into tractor work. As soon as we had a tractor, he bought ploughs and cultivators to it. He taught me how to start ploughing and I grew into that very quickly and continued all my life like that. We'd a little petrol, paraffin tractor to start with and a two-furrow plough. And then, as time went on, I got a bit bigger tractor and then I got a three furrow plough. It wasn't a very good plough really. It didn't make too good a job, but we got by with it. And then, after me father died, I came across a very good three furrow plough and that really made a nice job. And I've got a little bit bigger tractor since then. It's been

easy work for it and I've continued right to the present day using that one plough."

Adapting to the changing methods was not easy. Howard's father, unfamiliar with tractor work, would nevertheless know what should be done.

"He'd tell me what to do and show me how to go on. Of course when we got a tractor and this two-furrow plough, it was a bit different to ploughing with horses and a single-furrow. He told me what he could about ploughing, but he had to learn a bit as well. It made quite a lot of difference having to handle two furrows. Different altogether really. But he used to watch me and tell me what I'd done right and what I'd done wrong and then teach me all he knew."

Tractors grew in size and power.

"In the late 1930's the old Standard Fordson came into being on farms. And then the two-furrow plough. Of course it speeded the job up quite a bit. A chap could go with his tractor and his two furrow plough and he'd probably plough three acres, might be four, in a day if the going went well. He was riding on the tractor instead of walking behind it and that made things a lot easier.

And then, after that, later models came out ..... the big tractors came, the four-wheel drive tractors and they could pull an eight-furrow reversible plough, and they are capable of doing 50 or 60 acres a day. So it was a big advance and it cut all the labour out. Instead of a dozen men working, there'd be one man on this big tractor. And all the time, the labour force was dwindling on the farms and so in a way, it spoilt the friendliness of the job, because you were working on your own and loneliness 'd creep in then. I think the last, the biggest plough I've ever seen .... I went to a demonstration one time .... it was a fourteen-furrow plough and there were eight furrows on one frame and then behind that there was another frame with six furrows on it. And a massive crawler tractor, I think it was 450 horse power, pulling this lot and they could cover 70 or 80 acres in a day. And it was just mass production then."

Howard ploughing at Dale Bank Farm, Milltown.

Ploughing was often cold work.

"One time, (I think it'd be when we'd taken the kale and cabbages off, so it'd be getting late into December) we had to finish this field. We should have drilled some of it earlier on, after we'd got mangolds and potatoes off and put wheat in there. Then we should have to wait till we'd cleared all the kale off before we could finish the field. It was nearly Christmas time, I'd almost finished drilling and it started snowing. And that was it till after the snow had gone. Several weeks after, the wheat was showing up. It had grown under the snow, the snow had insulated it.

But <u>we</u> weren't insulated. Not in them days. It was a case of put plenty of clothes on, and a pair of gloves, and you let your feet freeze. You're not working any circulation up at all. You're just sitting. Luckily, with that old David Brown tractor, you had quite a lot of protection from the weather, there was a cowling in front of you and also you got warmth from the engine blowing back at you. It did help quite a lot. It shielded your hands on the steering wheel. You didn't get quite so cold as on some of these exposed tractors. Some of 'em, there was nothing to protect you at all. Ah, folks were glad of the old Army great coats that came onto the market. They'd keep you a bit warmer. The previous generation wore leather leggings fastened with a strap and a buckle, top and bottom. They went just over the top of the heavy boots and that's all they had to keep their legs dry. We used Wellingtons and ordinary raincoats. The Wellingtons were rubber, quite soft and comfortable. Odd times, if it was raining, you'd tuck one corner of a hessian sack into the other corner and it would form a hood. It would keep your head and shoulders a bit dry, for a while but they'd not keep you very dry. Your arms'd get wet.

I should usually come home for my dinner, but sometimes, if I was ploughing on Brown Lane, I should take my dinner with me, if it wasn't too bad weather. I should just take some sandwiches and a flask of tea. Of course, when I was contracting during the war, I should have to take sandwiches and a drink with me. Some days, they weren't too warm. I used to warm my hands on exhaust pipe because they'd got that cold I'd a job to feed myself. I used to huddle down at the side of my tractor – leave engine running so it kept warm and sit with my back to engine where it was a bit warmer.

That's something the old horse and ploughmen couldn't do, but at least they were walking all the time, keeping them warm. Their hands'd be frozen, though, holding plough stilts, although they were wooden. The ploughmen were completely exposed to the elements and their fingers weren't doing anything particular, only gripping these wooden stilts. Because the horses would follow the furrow and, if they were well trained, they'd turn into the next furrow and you hardly need to steer them with reins. They'd know the job. You'd got to hold the plough and drag it about. Oh, you'd certainly keep warm, doing that job."

Ploughing could be difficult, even dangerous, work both with horses and tractors.
"The old fellows sometimes got broken ribs with the plough shafts. If the horse were going pretty well and pulling well and the plough hit a solid stone, it'd throw the stilts up – they call them plough stilts, the handles. And, if they swung up

ever so hard and hit him on his ribs, odd times they'd break ribs with the impact. They used to dread hitting a stone.

And tree roots, that was another nasty thing. The plough'd go under a tree root and probably wedge, then he'd have to try and drag it back and get it freed again. I remember, when I was tractor ploughing, I first started off with a trailer plough, before hydraulic ploughs, ploughing these grass fields up during the war and invariably, there'd be trees all round the outside and particularly ash trees. Their roots, they'd go into the field, oh! 20 yards, 30 yards you'd start encountering ash tree roots. And as you got closer to the side you got thicker and thicker roots till they'd be as thick as my leg. And I can remember the plough'd jam under a tree root and I should have to unhitch the tractor from the front, go round the back and hang a chain on and pull it out, backwards, from under this root. Oh! it was a terrible job. Of course, with hydraulic ploughs, the plough's attached to the tractor and you just reverse your tractor, lift your plough up and go over it. Made it a lot easier then, if you didn't break your plough! That could happen. You bent your plough all shapes. Eh dear! There was hardly one decent hydraulically mounted plough, in the early days, that wasn't twisted and bent through that job. Because the tractor didn't stop. It kept pulling and something had to give way. Eh! I've spent many a day straightening me plough out, taking parts off it and straightening them out and trying to make it work. That's why, many a time at ploughing matches, my plough didn't run as well as it should do because it had been twisted."

Ideally, ploughing should be finished before Christmas. This was to allow a frost mold – the hard frosts would occur after Christmas – to break the soil down into a fine tilth by the spring. If there hadn't been frost action ploughing would be such hard work that the horses would get harness-sore. Even with a tractor the lack of frost can still make cultivation difficult.

THE FARMING YEAR: SOWING AND GROWING

With the ground well broken down, it would be time to manure it.
The job was fitted into the daily routine whenever possible.

"In the old days, every chance that they had, they'd have to be
getting some muck carted out either on to grass land or
stubble. It'd all be horse work of course, a very slow job.
They'd fill this cart by hand in the yard at the muck heap.
Then take it out into the field and they had what they called
a muck drag. It was a long shaft with a three-pronged fork on
the end at right angles. They'd pull the muck out of the cart
with this muck drag and leave it in heaps, perhaps a couple
of barrows full in a heap. And then they'd draw on a bit
further and drop another heap till they'd empty the cart. And
then, when they'd done this muck-carting business like that,
any odd times when the weather was bad or freezing or it was
raining, a chap'd go and spread these heaps of muck by hand
and that's how they got rid of it. It was a slow, laborious job.
And then, as spring approached, they'd probably start and
plough this muck in on the stubble ground then."

The animal manure would be broken down by weather and time.
When spring came, fertilizer was spread on the ground. Usually,
nowadays, Howard puts on about two hundredweight per acre. In
earlier times perhaps only about one hundredweight to an acre
would be put on; it was done by hand. Manure provides bulk, but
chemical fertilizers are needed as well.

"Your ordinary muck provides a humus as well as
nutrients in your soil but fertilizer, it just tops the
nitrogen and potash and phosphates up. When we used to
grow roots that ground was mucked very heavily: 25 tons to
the acre of muck on it. It was plastered thick and ploughed in.
And even then, we should sow some fertilizers on, to add to it.
Then, after we'd got that crop off, we always used to put
wheat on that ground, the following year. And we should
never need any fertilizer or muck on that field because there'd
be so much left in the soil and it carried through to another
year.
One kind of fertilizer was basic slag. This was the end

product from the steel smelting mills, a waste product from the furnace. It was crushed, just like flour, and it was a dirty, sooty black – horrible stuff – and as heavy as lead. A little bag'd weigh ten stone. They were hessian bags and the slag was so fine, it'd riddle out and we were as black as soot. We used to tip it into the drill and spread it. It was very good for the grassland. The chemicals in it were beneficial for good quality grass. It's never used now, there's no slag to be obtained. I think we fetched it from Stretton Station. The sacks were very strong and woven fine, but every time you touched them, the slag would puff out. It was a filthy job, even tipping it into the drill, the dust shot up and your clothes, your hands, your face were covered. At that time there were no compound fertilisers, I think we had some stuff called sulphate of ammonia – some of that'd go on corn ground as well, and nitre chalk was another one. One year we had some stuff called North African rock phosphate that came to Stretton Station in two hundred weight bags. We had a job lugging it out of a covered railway wagon onto our little dray."

In the meantime seed would have been ordered. Turnip, mangold and kale seed would come by post in little hessian bags. Or, if Mr Davison had saved his own seed, it would need to be tested.

"Very often me father used to have a plate with some blotting paper on it and keep it moist. He went to the trouble of counting a hundred seeds onto the blotting paper and he'd see how many eventually sprouted and then he'd got the percentage germination. Because he'd sow his own seed. I can remember him having this blotting paper wet on a plate.

Before we had the drill, my father used to sow fertilizer by hand – a hopper in front of him. It's a heavy job, tramping round the field. He sowed acres and acres with a hopper. It would hold two or three stone. You knew you'd got that hanging round your neck when it was full of fertilizer. In fact me father used to sow small seeds out of it, grass seed, before he had a seed fiddle. And that'd be finger and thumb. You'd

THE OFFICIAL SEED TESTING STATION

No. D 9689   HUNTINGDON ROAD, CAMBRIDGE.

20th Feb. 1938

Received _the sum of_ 2/- _in respect of_ Deposit a/c Fees _for testing_ 1 _samples._

Ref No. Cc-3440

Amount of fees...... 2/-

Balance due ....

Balance credited ....

ALFRED EASTHAM,

Chief Officer.

Per

Mr B Davison. Dale Bank Fm. Ashover. Chesterfield.

only need to pick that quantity of seed out with your finger and thumb, not get a handful, like you would with fertilizer. He thought he'd really got something when he got a seed fiddle."

Seed sowing was another job that Olive's father could do.

"He liked his beer. But apart from that he could be a wonderful worker. He was a chap of this sort, that he could put his hand to anything. Stone wall building you know, and all that kind of a thing. And when they were seeding a field they used to put, what they called a hopper, round their neck and it was like a big thing in front of them. And I've

There's her Dad.

seen him go up and down. And it's wonder he didn't drop, up and down this field, striding it out. Must have gone miles and miles doing that. And he'd be throwing so much that way with this hand and that way wi' that hand. Oh ah, that's how they used to set seed. He'd do the whole field by himself."

And, although she did not use it herself, Miss Bassett remembers seeing seed set with a sowing fiddle.

"You moved a thing round and as you walked along you left a trail of seed behind. You'd got it fixed on your body some way or other. I can't remember how. The horse binder and those implements had come into fashion when I first began to be interested."

A gardener might grow roots to feed a farmer's animals, Walter Hopkinson remembers that he had

"A little garden plough you could set seeds with too. It was made by ATCO, a firm in Derby. There were different sized holes on the wheel hub so you sowed your seed according to size. I bought it at a big pub between Alfreton and Wessington (the Butcher's Arms) for £6. I used to grow turnips and mangolds and let Tommy Outram have them for the cattle."

Even with the seed fiddle, sowing grass seed would be a very slow process for it didn't sow wide. Howard's father would start at four in the morning. The job was made more difficult because it was almost impossible to see where you had walked. (When you are using a tractor and seed drill, the tractor wheelmarks are a guide.) The solution for someone like Howard's father in earlier years was to work towards stakes pushed in at the hedge side and move them down the field as the sowing progressed. Now Howard uses a fertilizer spreader to sow grass seed. This spreads a strip about ten foot wide at a time. His father's work was made much easier when he bought a drill. With one such machine:

"You'd ridge the ground up with a ridge plough and then rollers would run on that ridge and the seed'd drop in and the roller would squash it down. Our drill – there's one roller there and another one follows behind. This front roller forms a rounded ridge, the coulter drills the seed and the second roller solidifies your row where the seed's gone in, rolls it in and compresses it. The little turnip drill had a shaped roller at the back to bury its seed a bit, but we always went over it with a flat roller after, to consolidate the ground and help germination.

We'd another drill, it had discs which were half exposed at the back and as they went round a shutter opened up and down on the middle of the discs and allowed so much fertilizer or whatever on to the disc. And on the exposed part of the disc there's a little spinning disc with either two or three little prongs sticking out on it. And that used to spin very fast and flick out whatever was on these discs. That was a very efficient drill. We used that for a long time."

The great drawback with this drill was that it was extraordinarily difficult to manoeuvre.

"It was about nine feet wide and you couldn't get it through our gateways at that time. You had to man-handle it through. You'd back up to the gateway and you'd shove one wheel through to the outside and then bring the other one through after it. That's how we used to work through gates. They took some working through on your own. I shall never forget that field up Stubben Edge of ours, and there was an old chap lived in that bungalow. I'd got to get this drill out of that gateway right at the top corner against this bungalow, and he was sat watching me as I struggled to get this drill through the narrow gateway and he says "I do like to see folks working!"

This drill was useful also for putting on a protection for the emerging seedlings. They were liable to attack from flea beetles which nipped off the roots. One year, in an attempt to stop them, Howard's father dragged sacks soaked in tar over the rows. This may have been effective but it was "a right messy job" and as an alternative, lime dust was used.

"We used to have to go with a bucket, scattering this lime-stone dust. When we bought the drill we had perhaps a couple of ton of limestone dust tipped up at the corner of the field and I had to shovel it into this drill and go up and down these turnip rows, spreading it on that way. Later on, I remember me father mixing these turnip seeds in a tin and putting either a powder or a liquid on the seed and stirring it up prior to drilling it and that protected them against the flea beetle."

This particular insect is no longer a pest because nowadays the seed is dressed.

"On the bigger scale, we seem to have been able to control pests and diseases. There's always been some chemical that we could put on to destroy the predators in corn. They reckon the earlier you plant corn – a lot of farmers are planting in September or late August even – the more prone it is to diseases in the winter. Then they have to spray against these diseases, that's how they're controlling them now. When I've set wheat, I've never planted it before middle of October right through till November and it doesn't seem to have been affected as badly with soil-borne diseases. I don't know why. You'd think, earlier it was planted and a stronger crop before winter set in, it would be better, but it seems to encourage insects and pests to attack it more. Big arable farms, they're spraying all year round – as soon as they've planted an

DEPÔT FOR
Ucal
SPECIALITIES.

TELEPHONE No. 40.

Market Street, Clay Cross,
Oct 18 1927

To E. G. Holmes, M. P. S.

Pharmacist,

PATENT AND FAMILY MEDICINES, FANCY SOAPS, PERFUMERY, &c.
PRESCRIPTIONS ACCURATELY DISPENSED.
KODAK AND ALL PHOTOGRAPHIC SUPPLIES.

1/0 Copper Sulphate — 8

For dry
Wheat
Dressing

Recd with thanks
E. G. Holmes

autumn crop, they spray it with a pre-emergence spray, to stop weeds growing and then there'll be a fungicide spray. Then in spring, there'll be some more sprays applied to it and they even spray some crops just before they combine now, to kill any weeds off. I don't think it affects the actual grain at all. ....Of course, years ago, we'd severe frosts in winter and that did a lot to get rid of weeds and pests."

Seed sowing nowadays is both easier physically and less stressful to the mind.

"They're not the old country folks who they used to be, watching farmers at work. The folks around now, they couldn't care less about farmers, what they're sowing. We were afraid of being teased if it looked a bit rough. All the old natives, they'd watch it and see if there was a bit missing and they'd not forget to remind you. I know one year I drilled me corn and, I didn't know it, but the mechanism that fed the seed coming out of me drill, it had worn and worn till a cog kept missing teeth. And I didn't know that had happened. And when me crop came up there'd be patches all over the field where this cog had stopped turning. There'd happen be five or ten yards that nothing'd come. Drill had stopped feeding corn – a bare patch. Oh, that field, it did look a disgrace, bare patches all over it. I was glad when I'd harvested crop off that. I was sick of looking at it. Then I found out what had happened and I mended me drill up before next time.

Course me drill, it came over to this country in 1940 from America on lease-lend. A big farmer at Pentrich had it new and when he was finished with it me father bought it and I tidied it up where it had been worn and I'm still using it now. Ah, that's done good service. And when corn comes up it looks just as good as this corn that folks have put on with a big, expensive drill. They are ever so expensive and so complicated. I know they take a lot wider width when they're in the field, but some of them, they've a huge hopper on – it'll hold a ton of seed and from their hopper there's a pipe comes to every coulter. And it looks like a great big octopus. Ah, there must be twenty or thirty of these pipes all come out of the bottom of this big hopper and they reckon seed's blown through with compressed air! There's a great big fan fitted to it somewhere to blow it through. What a complicated thing to drill a bit of corn! Then, to go to the other extreme, a farmer I know puts his on with a fertilizer spreader and disc harrows it and he gets his crop about the same."

After the corn was planted, it was time to set other seeds: mangolds and turnips and kale and potatoes. These needed different treatment.

"That land had to be mucked very heavily. All the spare muck that we'd got in the place was carted on to the land for these root crops, pulled out in heaps, spread by hand and then ploughed in again. Then there was the laborious job of working the root ground down which was a lot worse than the corn ground because it'd got to be a very fine deep loose mold. It'd be cultivated, and perhaps rolled and cultivated again and rolled again to break all the lumps down and get it nice and fine. And then we would go with a couple of horses and a ridge plough and draw it up into long rows. And, when it was dry enough, then we'd go with a turnip drill and drill the mangold seed or turnip seed and then roll the rows down.

After that it'd be potato planting and that was all hand work as well. You'd draw these rows up and you'd go with a bucket full of potatoes, and drop them in at every ten or twelve inch interval along these rows. And when you'd done that, the horses came with this ridge plough and split these ridges and covered the potatoes up that way. And that's how they were planted. Of course the other rows, they were left for mangolds and turnips and kale. We'd a little turnip drill that ran on these ridges, pulled with a horse again, and that drilled the seed and that was all rolled in."

There was another way of doing potatoes.

"They ridged these rows up and then they'd put muck in the rows and spread it down the rows. And then, in that instance, the chap'd get in the cart and he'd chuck it out in forkfuls into these rows, as evenly as he could, and then they used to go what they called "muck knocking." They'd go with a fork and level all this muck down in the bottom of the rows, and then they planted the potatoes in the muck. And then ridged them up again and covered them up with a ridge plough. And that was another way of planting potatoes.

And then after that, everything was set and we were waiting for it to grow."

As the crops begin to grow they are liable to be attacked by various pests.

"The rats, they'll be in a corn field, oh yes, they'll be in. As soon as there's any grain they'll be there. And you can get crows. If they can start on a bit of a laid patch, they'll keep flattening it down and eating the grain and ah! they can flatten big areas. If a bit of a patch gets laid down, crows'll descend on that patch and they'll shove the rest down and keep eating and eating at the grain and a big flock of crows can flatten huge areas. Sometimes crows can take the grain out when you've drilled it. When it's just starting to show through, crows find it and they'll follow the drill down and eat the grain out. They once wiped a crop out for me – about a three-acre field. They dug down with their beaks and found the grain and then they followed it down the drill mark and kept eating it as they went along. And there'd be two or three hundred in a flock of crows; the whole field, it can be black over with crows. It's almost too late if you don't notice, if you don't see the field every day. It wasn't worth leaving that field – I had to drill it again.

I think of one field, a long time ago, that got practically wiped out with leather jackets. They eat the shoot off just below ground level and you suddenly notice a lot of it starting to die off and you get hold of a shoot and you pull it out and

it's severed from its root. They clear a field out in a few days, they've got a good start before you notice. At that time we'd got a chemical called dieldrin and we sprayed that on and that killed them off. There were all these dead leather-jackets on surface and the crows came and ate 'em all. The field was covered in crows for a couple of days while they were feeding off the dead leather-jackets. I don't know if it affected the crows or not, but of course this dieldrin has been banned.

Of course, if you could shoot an odd crow or two and hang it up in the field, that'd keep 'em off. They didn't like to see any dead crows lying about. It worked over a period of a few days but then they'd gradually get braver and come in again. If you kept shooting a few and hanging them up, it'd put 'em off a bit. I remember once I were ploughing and I was absolutely smothered in seagulls. There were hundreds of them following my plough. And I shot one or two, well, I only had one shot and there was about three or four, they were that close together. And I just threw them out over ploughing and I never had another seagull. Trouble was, fox took all dead 'uns, you've got to start again.

Moles, they were a pest. They were dealt with by a man and his son, lived at Moorwood Moor and it was their job, they did nothing else, only mole catching. They used to come round on a yearly basis to farms and they used poison. They had worms in, probably strychnine, I don't know. And they used to drop these worms into these mole runs and that's how they used to wipe 'em out. But next year there'd be some more moles. They never stopped 'em. There was always some moles. But these mole-catcher chaps, they didn't live very long, and we reckoned it was through handling this strychnine on a daily basis, that it finished 'em off. Of course, there were other mole-catchers who used traps but they seemed to disappear. I suppose they couldn't get a living at the job. I vaguely remember one of these old chaps coming round with a great bundle of mole traps hung over his shoulder.

As soon as mangolds and turnips and kale started showing through in the rows, the weed was there as well and you had to start weeding. We'd a one horse hoe that used to go up and down these rows. That took the bulk of the weeds out between the rows and then the final stage was go by hand hoe and hoe

Wingerworth Park,
Chesterfield,

........*March*........19*30*

M*r*...... *Davidson* ....

Dr. to A. ALLWOOD,

MOLE CATCHER.

					s	d
For destroying Moles.					°	*d*
on 4 0 acres						
@ 1*d* per acre					3	4
Rec*d* with thanks						
A. Allwood						

all round the plants and chop them out at eight or nine inch intervals, leaving little bunches of plants. Then it was singling by hand and you crawled up and down the rows on your hands and knees and separated these bunches till there was one plant left. That was a miserable job, crawling on your hands and knees up these rows, singling turnips and mangolds. I can remember doing that with sacking tied round me knees to stop them getting sore with kneeling on the ground, and perhaps wet as well, because they were not always dry seasons. We should be doing it in rain. And when you'd finished singling, there'd be weed growing in the middle

of the rows again, so you'd have to go through with the horse
hoe again. Every spare minute we were going hoeing weeds in
the root ground. And you did that, by hand of course, till the
next thing was hay-making time coming up."

THE FARMING YEAR: HAY-MAKING

For labour intensive jobs on the farm a farmer often drew on outside help. In the 1930s such work would be welcome as a source of
extra income. Howard describes the busyness of hay-making. His
words blend with the mingled voices of some of the people who
helped on farms at this time.
  "Hay-making, we shouldn't be just on our own. We should
  have one or two fellows come and help to cart it in regularly."

Olive comes to the point:
  "Anybody did it that they could rope in."

  "We used to have an old colliery chap from Tupton and he
  really used to enjoy coming and doing a job on the farm for us
  at Dale Bank. He'd do his shift down the pit and then he'd
  come up to us and have another three or four hours helping
  us. He was a big strong chap. He really enjoyed the fresh air.
  Yes, it were nice to get outside and do a different job. There
  was labour anywhere you could pick out to help you a bit."

Miss Bassett's memory is long:
  "Of course, in summer time, there were none of the modern
  hay-making appliances. The fields were all done by hand."

The grass would be cut with scythes – a job which Miss Bassett
tackled.
  "Well, I had several tries, but I never became very expert at
  it. I think I was too dangerous. I think I would have cut somebody's leg off if I had had to do very much of it. But we
  employed people to do it and I can remember it being done."

With time though came "modern" implements.
  "Well, we thought we were very up to date when we got a

horse-mowing machine, rather than this old-fashioned scythe. But I wasn't particularly mechanically minded, so I didn't take much interest in that part. I left the modern gadgets to the youngsters."

And, as Margaret Graney recalls, the equipment had to be maintained. To prepare for hay-making, her father rested the blade of the mowing machine across the tops of two walls and would spend a whole day sharpening it.

"So you started, says Howard, the horses hung on to a mowing machine and you mowed a field of grass. The trouble was that with the horse rake – you've nothing to stop you falling off. It's not a safe place, because you're so high up, to start with. On a mowing machine you're low down. But on that thing, you're liable to fall on the rake itself. Oh, there were no Health and Safety in them days. If you fell off, it was your own fault. On rare occasions, the horse'd bolt and leave

Mowing the hay.

you behind. You'd fall off behind very likely.

After you've mown with the horse-mower, there's always a bit left round the outside that you can't mow with a mowing machine. So, in those days, that mustn't be left. It had got to be cut. So we went with a scythe and we hobbed it out. That's where the term "hobbing out" comes from: mowing the grass round the outside of the field with a scythe, that the mowing machine can't touch. And so the binder could finish the last width by going the other way round the field and cutting a back swath."

Ted Hellaby's diary
  23 Sept 1931. Mown wall side out round Barn field."

It was different for the corn crop as John Heathcote says.
"But you always cut the corn <u>before</u> you went round. Made a road round it."

Howard's mother
"used to mow with the horse mower and she would have to scythe the edges and then gather up the hay with a bonny rake. That is a big wide rake. It'd be about five feet wide and it's all lightish wood. The shaft curves down to the head and there's a row of wooden teeth, like a hand rake, only the teeth are long, and they're the full length of the head. You drag it behind you, this bonny rake, and you'd the handle up here and the handle comes down, then it splits into two and where it forks out, there's a hand grip and top handle's here. You walk with it behind you and it rakes up the scattered hay that's been left behind after the main crop's been lifted off. Me mother used to walk miles with that thing, when they were hay-making, – dragging that behind her. Because we should rake the full crop up with a horse rake, and that'd be in long rows. And then we should go with a hay cart and we should pick it up loose at that time, with hand forks, on to cart. And of course, you couldn't scratch every bit up so she'd come after us with this bonny-rake, raking all the loose bits up. And when she'd got a rake full, she'd just draw it into where we were loading and then set off again. Eeh, she went miles with that bonny-rake."

Not without aggravation, for:

"Her father used to get on to her about raking this swath out. he used to say that if it wasn't done right, they couldn't mow round and those who rake out want to have to mow as well, for them to make a proper job of it. And that's how they used to go on in those days. It was hard work then, for her, but that was the accepted thing. You didn't have anything else and you wanted to collect every bit of hay up that you could. You didn't want any waste at that time."

"It was hard work, but we didn't know anything different." Millie Ablett explains.

It was vital work too, as was explained to Miss Lennox in a most matter-of-fact way.

"I went to a farm and I wanted some data for my records. The daughter and mother said, "Oh we can work that out because we mowed the big meadow when father died. And we said, we can't have the funeral until we've got the hay in". They told the vicar and the vicar said, "Well it's got to be within seven days". They said, "Well let's hope it's fine for seven days, then".

Joe Holmes, at this time was working part time on the farm and part time in the quarry. One of his jobs was mowing.

"Ah, quarries were on three days a week. I used to do other three days farming – for Mr Nightingale at Raven House. I used to bring horses up and turn 'em on Ashover Hay when I was coming back at night and call in the morning and take 'em back with me about four o'clock in the morning. I'd be mowing by five o'clock, as soon as it came daylight. Aye, they were long days, when you're mowing early in the morning till late at night."

This was a reflection of the hard times experienced during the Depression in agriculture in the 1930s. Joe continues:

"I've mowed with one of the old mowers, sat up high behind the horses. You'd got to watch what you were mowing all the time, that were trouble. If you got a rabbit, they used to get out of way of you. You'd not catch them. But if you got a mouse nest on one of the points it'd make it start missing. You'd be leaving a lot of grass behind. You'd got to watch all the time. Mouse nests were biggest trouble."

The mown grass lay in the field and then, as Millie Ablett says:
"When it wanted getting ready, you had to go out and shake it with a fork – and you'd just get it ready and it'd rain, oh dear! Then weather'd perhaps take up again and then you had to go and shake it out again. Then you'd have turner in to fluff it up again and dry it better."

"Very often," Howard agrees, "we used to turn it by hand, two or three of us with a hay-rake and we'd turn a field of grass like that. It was a slow job and I know sometimes we should start turning and by the time we'd just turned it, it was going to rain and that would finish the job off again for a day or two. Then you shook it all out again and hoped it dried then."

Ted Hellaby's diary
    June 1931 " Turned Browsey Field with Monty."

The hay, once mown would be left to dry, as Joe explains.
"Mow it and leave it, then turn it next day. You go round w' hay rake, raking it into heaps."

It did not dry evenly Millie Ablett points out:
"Round by the hedges it was always wetter so you had to shake that out individually by hand because the sun didn't get to the edges."

A watchful eye was needed though. Harry Towndrow
"once got up at three a.m. to go to Church Town, Darley Dale, with a couple of other men. We were up there and we'd cocked it up at Saturday night. It weren't ready then but it were hot weather and it had "made". It was on the point of getting too dry. We thought "We'll not be able to pick it up if it gets that dry.""

Preparation could avert any possible rain damage, as Fred Hole explains.

"You cut the grass, turned it and then cocked it up. You'd got
to cock it up nicely. You hadn't got to shove it up in a heap,
that's hopeless. My uncle at Old Engine (he'd got over 100
acres) when he'd cocked it all up he'd top these cocks to keep
water out. They used to make a cap out of grass, you'd get so
much on a fork, a thick layer, level it and he wopped it over,
there was a certain way of doing it, onto the cock. It were like
an umbrella."

Howard is philosophical – practical:
"But that's how we carried on. It was best though to turn the
hay the least possible number of times, for each time it was
turned some of it disappeared and some volume was lost. And
if it did come a bit wet and we couldn't go hay-making we
went back in the turnip field and hoed weeds out."

In those days the work was done with pride. Men valued their tools
for they enabled them to give a professional and solid finish to
their work as Joe explains.
"Farmer's always got plenty of forks. Some men had their own
but you weren't forced to. Some men'd use no fork only their
own. Ah, they were very suspicious about that job. A lot of
these farm lads always got their own fork – wouldn't let anybody else use it."

This was because these implements were "tailor made". Some were
longer and some had shorter shafts so they suited their individual
owners. Joe, though, borrowed a fork because he couldn't afford
one of his own.

Machinery was a great help.
"Then came the difficult task of deciding whether the hay,
lying in swaths down the field, was ready to be gathered and
stored. Two swaths would be gathered into one windrow. We
used to feel at it – get some in our hands and feel at it – see
if we thought it was dry enough. It was really experience that
gave you the idea that it was ready for carting in. I know,
when me father died, (I'd always relied on him) I felt in an
awful mess because I'd got this hay-making to do and I didn't
know how to judge whether it was going to be fit to store or

"Ah, that's me father on the swath-turning machine. They're turning the swath there, it turned two swaths at once, that thing did. There's a set of tines there, then another set of tines almost behind where he's sitting, on the other side. It spans two swaths, and that dark object there, that's a sheet of tin that stops these tines throwing this swath on to top of another one. It stops it throwing it too far, and then, there'll be another tin in between the two wheels, to stop the other swath being thrown on to top of this one. You pulled that with a horse and it turned the swaths and then you'd per - haps turn it again and if you were lucky it'd be dry enough to rake up into rows."

not. I felt so scared that it might not be right when I got it in. It was a bit of a catchy job. As long as the weather's settled, you don't mind, but when there's rain coming, you think to yourself "Shall I risk it and get it in before it's ready or shall I leave it and hope it doesn't get spoilt?"

"Catchy weather" meant hard decisions. Sometimes you came off all right and another time you'd a heap of wet spoilt hay in the field. It's mainly experience, because crops differ so much. You can get a rye grass crop that dries out very quick and soon goes into hay – it's a coarse grass. And then if you get something with any clover in it, you never really know when it's fit to get in – because clover can soon make it "give again" (go back again to moist grass) and if you get that in a stack, it can overheat and cause no end of trouble.

"They're loading the hay." Young Howard Davison sits with his dog and behind him are Tom and Ben Towndrow with the cart. On the right "That's me father with the sling gear horse - when they got a load on and they're pulling up hill home they hang that horse in front of that one in the shafts. The long chains go back to the shafts on the dray and there's two horses on, to pull up the hill."

This is exactly what happened one year.

"I remember, I should only be a young lad and it'd be when we employed labour. We got this hay "nesh" as they called it – it's not quite dry enough – and it was stacked loose under our barn. It started to heat up and me father got that worried, he cut a hole down from the top, with a cutting knife, a circular hole. He cut down into the middle of the stack and fetched all this hot hay out to try and cool it down because he was frightened of it getting on fire. But normally we were safe. They say that hay in bales doesn't fire like it does in a loose stack because it's all compressed. It'll still get hot, very hot, but there isn't the air there to fire it. I've seen bales that've been overheated and they've gone a chocolatey colour, but they've never fired."

At that time, Millie Ablett explains,
"It was all loaded loose on big drays. They'd have a sling-gear horse then, to help to cart it."

Joe describes the skill needed to load a cart with hay. There would be three men pitching the hay up onto the cart:
"Three happen. One chap on top, making sure corners were solid, so it wouldn't fall off, so it'd ride. If you didn't make it solid you'd get half a load on, it'd all fall off. That was the big art in loading a dray properly. You had to make sure you'd got all your corners solid. Then solid in middle, solid all way through. Else, when it was travelling, it'd shake off. If you loaded it poorly, it'd go anywhere."

A mechanical hay loader would be a great advantage:

A hay loader and 1940 Fordson tractor. Moving spikes on the loader carried the hay onto the load. Howard says "We bought a hay loader and that was hitched behind a trailer. It picked the hay up and dropped it on to the trailer and there was one chap there, he positioned it, and stacked it on the trailer. You'd got to go very slow with the tractor of course, but it saved a lot of hand work. Then we carted that back home and put it under hay barn."

"We had what they called a picker in the hay barn. It was a big fork on a pulley and rope. You stuck the big fork into a load of hay and then, this rope went around pulleys and at the

MILLTOWN, ASHOVER,

July 1st 1932.

Mr. B. Davison

DR. TO T. W. WILLMOT,

SHOEING & GENERAL SMITH.

£ - s - d

1932		£	s	d
Mar 1.	Irons put on S. tree, 1 hook & side piece to Harrow		2	.
21.	2 old shoes.		2	.
Apr.12.	1 hook, 1 link, new handle rod		1	9
June.4.	1 clip to horse hoe		1	.
	handle piece to trolley		1	.
14	New shaft to manure fork		1	6
17	1 gall oil, 2 mac. files		4	6
	1 grey stone, 1 quarry stone		2	9
18	1 fork shaft. 4. 6in. 1 shaft 5ft.		2	6
21.	2 new shoes, 2 old shoes		5	6
23.	1 fork shaft 6ft		1	6
	1 shackel, 1 pin, 1 cotter to picker		1	.
		£ 1	7	.

Received July 29th 1932
T. W. Willmot
With Thanks.

other end, you'd a horse pulling it up. So it pulled a big lump of hay up onto this trolley in the roof of the hay-barn and then it ran along and you tripped this big heap of hay off where you wanted to drop it, on top of your hay stack and then spread it about there. The fork would be about four feet wide and about the length of my arms. And then at the bottom there were two steel blades turned upwards to grip the hay. The blades were pointing straight out when you pushed it into your load of hay and then you pulled a lever and it turned these blades across and they gripped it and held it together while you hauled it up. The horse would walk forward till he'd pulled it into place and then they'd lead him back again. Did he get bored doing that? I've no idea!

Oh, it saved some work, and you could have a long stack right under your hay barn and run this trolley along this rail and just drop your big forkfuls of hay anywhere you wanted. You could drop perhaps four big forkfuls before you even started to shift it, to spread it about. And then perhaps you'd stop unloading and go up, two of you (the chap who was using the horse and the one on the load) you'd both go up there and spread it out before you put some more on. Eventually, after we had no horses, I geared up a gadget that was driven with the tractor, like a drum that wound the rope on and we used that for quite a while."

The hot, dirty work called for refreshment. Joe reckons you could mow a field in a day.

"You'd have got five or six acres in before dinner. Then dinner in field. Ah."

The photograph shows the horse working a picker that was used in the field. The top of the picker (not shown on the photo) had pulley wheels. There was a further set of pulley wheels on the base (the upright pole which would be fixed to the ground.) The teeth holding the load of hay could be swung round to drop the load in the right place. When it was in position it was released by a catch at the side. This is different from the picker Howard describes where the pulley wheels worked on runners under the hay barn.

As Olive says

"Sometimes they took sandwiches, rather than break off. They'd have a cooked meal in evening when they'd done. I suppose they had to make the best of the weather."

A wife or mother would interrupt her busy schedule to take the midday meal into the field. A daughter might do this too. Margaret Graney, as a girl, would ride her elderly donkey, Charlotte, (if she could get her to go) down to the field where her father and the men were harvesting. The donkey had been ill-treated and hated men. Margaret would take the men a bottle of cold tea – the best thirst quencher. Joe remembers another welcome drink.

"Used to make their own beer, herb beer a lot of 'em did. Ah. Nettle beer. A lot of farm ladies used to make their own. My mother made some, ah."

"Oh yes" agrees Olive. "They used to make herb beer from nettles. At that hot, dry time of the year, they used to put it right under middle of a haystck to keep it cool, yes they did."

A similar refreshing thirst quencher was dandelion beer. Howard's mother used to make this.

"After the dandelions had been used once to make dandelion wine then she'd use the heads over again to make a beer out of it. It was a sort of a weak wine. I think she'd add perhaps lemons or oranges or something else to it, to add a bit more flavour, but it was a real nice refreshing drink. You could drink a pint of that and never suffer any ill-effects. And very often we should have that during harvest when we were working out in the field, have a drink of that, it was really nice."

A local farmer remembers that on one occasion not herb beer but real beer was provided, with a tragic result.

"Dad farmed at Littlemoor. When he was hay-making every-one would turn out with a hay fork to help. Beer was provided. One time two little boys found the beer while the men were working. One of them died from too much alcohol."

After dinner, once the hay was loaded onto the cart Joe would

"Start leading (that is, taking it to farm), from a different field. You'd be leading from a different field in afternoon. One that were mowed day or two before probably."

This would be the most exciting time for children, remembers Olive.

"Hay-making – we really used to clamber after a ride on hay cart."

And the day's work would only be finished, says Joe, when it went dark.

When the hay had been led into the yard it had to be stacked. First you would make the staddle by putting down brushwood and timber to protect it from the damp ground.

Ted Hellaby's diary
6 Oct 1931 " Made staddle for first stack.."

Leading a load of hay at Hilltop Farm July 1929.

Sometimes the work could be combined with pleasure. Bert Hopkinson describes how it was helped along at Revel Farm.

"We were one of the first to have a wireless in 1930. We installed a four valve set with a horn loud speaker. To change stations one had to change coils, 100 for Daventry, 75 for

North of England and 50 for the Midlands. It was powered by a large dry battery, a smaller dry battery and an acid filled accumulator. Music by Jack Payne, Henry Hall or Reginald Fort could be heard from half a mile away if it was turned up. At haymaking time my dad and his helpers could hear the cricket scores on the hay stack while unloading."

Olive has "Watched chap that used to live next door. He used to always have a stackyard, as they used to call it, and he used to put these big planks of wood and built stack on them to start with, to let air get underneath you see, and then when they'd as much as they'd got to put in it then they used to make it slope, like a roof, so that the rain would run off. When they'd got it into a hay stack, they used to thatch it then. Keep rain off it. Yes, I've seen my Dad do that. And they used to put pegs in, these thack pegs as they used to call them. They were wooden. And they used to drive 'em in, and then, I suppose, use string, proper string, to hold it down.

Well, they had to do that to keep it. It used to stand in good stead that did. Now, you see, they don't do anything like that, but they'd got to make a good job of it because it were their livelihood weren't it? Sometimes they used to put a cloth over

A neatly thatched stack at Dale Bank Farm, Milltown in 1929.

but not very often."

As Howard says, until the end of the war most of the work in hay-making was done by hand.

"Then these pick-up balers started to appear and that revolutionised hay-making. For a couple of years we had a contractor come and bale our hay and that made it easier for us. Then I got the idea I'd have a baler of my own. I think it was in 1952 or '53 that I got this second-hand baler and I was away contracting again with that, because I was one of the first with a baler and I did a tremendous amount of work, hay-baling for people all round this area. I remember once I was baling for George Bramley when he lived at Demonsdale. He was the blacksmith for the old Milltown quarry. It was a a field right at the top of Overton Drive beyond Overton Hall, heading out towards Slack. I felt a bit of a lurch as I was driving round. Next time, when I goes round, there's a great big mineshaft opened up. My baler wheel had pushed the top in and there was a great hole visible then."

And if, even with the help of the baler, the work might be too tiring Fred Hole remembers his remedy.

"We'd be doing it all day and then, when it come to about half past four the chap with me'd say, "Oh, I shall have to go milking." And I'd be left on my own. But one road of having a rest – if you chucked something onto baler quickly, it used to choke it and fetch belt off – and you could have a rest then!"

Joe comments disparagingly

"Ah. There's no work i' hay-making now is there? All machinery."

At the present time, more silage than hay is made. This has entailed changes in the crop that is grown.

"Wheat makes good silage, it's very high in protein. It has to be cut before it's really ripe, when the grain's in the milk stage. They never use clover now in a crop at all. A lot of it's this silage mixture. I don't know much about it because I've never made it. But evidently they don't seem to like clover in a silage mixture. It's all these fancy rye grasses they put in.

They talk about so much percentage dry matter and all the theory attached to it. It goes over my head now. We just went by experience. Ah, just making hay. That did for us. There seems to be such a lot of science involved in the job now, till it baffles you. The chaps that come and test this silage that they've got into the clamp specify so much percentage of this and so much percentage of that in it – and "you ought to have had a bit more of this in it and a bit more of that." It gets so confusing."

Joe Holmes remembers clover being grown alone as a crop.
"You never see no fields of clover now, like there used to be. There were whole fields of red clover and white clover. Made best hay, that did. But you don't see any now."

An experienced farmer could judge the type and quality of the hay to ensure that his milk cows had the most nutritious fodder. Howard explains:
"The grass cut in early June takes longer to dry, because it's so full of sap. They used to say there was nothing like some good June hay. It was full of nourishment, young grass. We used to try and get some June hay if we could. But it took such a lot of killing at that time because there was so much sap in it. Ah. When you got towards the end of July, the grass was starting to go dead. A bit of warm sun on it and it'd soon be hay. But it wasn't the good hay that you'd get earlier on. Late grass, when it's gone to seed, has lost its virtue.

The animals'd go for the June hay anytime. Ah. That we got at the end of July, we used to call it stirk hay because it was only fit for the young beasts. We never fed bad hay to milk cows. It was the young stock who had that, where it didn't matter so much. But milk cows, they wouldn't milk very well on bad hay. They had to have the best. And you could tell, if there was a bit of bad hay among some good hay, it'd be left in front of 'em at the end of the day. They wouldn't eat it. They'd sort it out."

And good management meant that
"We'd always enough fodder. We'd always a bit left when we turned the cows out the following summer. Ah, we were never

short of feed. Me father, I look back and I think he must have been a pretty good farmer. He could work things out quite well.

Ah, well, hay-making used to go on quite a long while. Depended a lot on the weather. If it was a good summer we should get through it fairly quick. Perhaps in a month or so, something like that, we should get it done. But I remember one year, it was a bad summer and we were still hay-making when the corn was ready to cut in August. It was a terrible summer that was. But eventually we should get through."

The Farming year: the corn harvest

By August, the corn – wheat, oats and barley would be ready for harvesting. Howard describes the process in some detail.

"Eventually we should get through the hay-making and the next thing, you'd be corn harvesting. And we should start bindering - cutting with binder and horses – and get the corn into sheaves, and stack these sheaves up in the field for them to dry out ready for carting home."

"They sometimes had three horses to pull a binder", adds Fred Hole.

"Before the combine harvesters we used to "open out" before cutting corn with a binder. That meant going round the out-side with a scythe to mow the first cut of corn, to give room for the horses, or tractor later, to go round with the binder. Otherwise they'd trample all the first lot down with their feet and machines and waste it all. Father'd get a pliable ash branch, and he'd fasten it to the bottom of his scythe and loop it round and bring it back and fasten it up there like a loop. It helped to sweep your corn up when you were cutting it. Otherwise, very often it'd fall back over your scythe blade.

You'd go with a scythe and the chap behind'd go with what he called a taking-up rake. That was a little steel rake with three longish times on it, and it'd only be about 15 to 18 inches wide. He'd follow the scythe with this rake, keep raking it towards him till he formed a sheaf, (a bundle of corn) with this rake and he'd keep raking it on to the instep of his foot till he got a sheaf bundled on to it. And then he put that

A reaper binder, or self-binder, at Hilltop Farm in 1930 with Beauty and Bess.

Opening out for cutting corn.

to one side and, if there were two of 'em, the other chap would make a band out of straw. And he'd join the heads together, because the straw perhaps wouldn't be long enough to go right round the sheaf on its own, so he'd need a double length. The heads were twisted round in a certain fashion, to hold together and he'd put the straw band round the sheaf and then it'd be twisted and tucked under to hold it in place and then he'd got the sheaf formed and tied up. If there was only one chap doing the taking-up he'd take up with his rake till he got perhaps four or five bundles and then he'd go back and tie them up and then go on again. When you were tying the bands, oat straw got very long, you'd probably make the band out of a single length of straw, and some wheat'd perhaps be the same. Barley straw was short and softer, you could make a band out of it, but it wouldn't be as long."

Howard used a combined reaper binder.

"Mine had a right hand cut which was rare. It cut the corn and then a canvas elevator at the side takes it up and down

Howard and his father corn cutting.

An old sail reaper, photographed in 1905.
This kind of reaper went out of use long before Howard's time.

to the knotter at the other side. That bundles it up into sheaves. Then it brings a string round it and ties it and throws it out as a sheaf. And then we used to collect these sheaves and stack them up in eights, four each side to form a triangular piece to run the rain off. The ends would be left open to allow the air to circulate. The proper name for these is "stooks". We just called 'em stacks. "We're going stacking up."

The machinery developed over the years.
"The old horsedrawn reaper was a mowing machine. Then, behind the cutter bar there were slats, the corn fell onto them. A chap sat on the machine with a long fine toothed rake. As there got enough corn onto the slats to make a sheaf he raked it off."

John Heathcote worked with one of these:
"There was a big wide wheel on the old reaper and the seat was on something that went over the wheel. There were a flat

A reaper binder in use with a Fordson tractor.
Ernest Smith and son Arthur on board at Woodthorpe Grange.

bed, slats, on that. You sat on this seat and you drove your horses round and you pulled the corn back as you'd cut it. You kept pulling it back onto the bed with your rake and then, when you thought you'd got enough on there to make a sheaf, you lifted your foot off this pedal and it let the bed go down, and then you put rake on it and, as you were going, just kept pushing it off each time you'd got enough for a sheaf. You'd have about half a dozen people following you round, making bands out of straw and tying 'em up.

If you were cutting it with a reaper, and you were cutting big fields, you needed about six or eight men all the time, to keep the machine going round. If you were doing it right, you could keep this bloke going round with horses and reaper, all time, pushing 'em off and others were just picking it up, bundling it up and tying – you made bands. You pulled your straw out of the sheaf, straightened it out, two lengths, wrapped heads together and fastened 'em up with bands of straw. No string like, then.

When reaper and binder combined come in it did away with old fashioned reaper.

After the corn was cut with the reaper binder, you had to stack the sheaves up in eights, and they had to be facing north-south, so as the sun could get on both sides. When I worked at Slack, my uncle was away delivering milk until about two o'clock and he got on to us one day, he says "You've not got 'em all north and south." We thought we had and one of the sons, who was still at school, went and fetched a compass."

Miss Basset recalls
"They said that when the field of corn was cut, it should stand in those stooks, drying and hear the church bells ring for three Sundays."
"Then we children used to play hide and seek underneath them." Eva Butler recalls.

Howard reflects that the corn harvest was enjoyable work.
"In those days, anybody'd come and help us. We should perhaps have four or five people come in and help us with corn harvest. And it was a happy pastime – everybody was talking and telling tales and laughing and news came in from other quarters. It was entertaining and time passed a lot quicker that way, when there was a lot of you about. It was quite a nice job when it was dry but odd times, when we've cut a field with the binder and before we could get stacking up, it'd come a thunderstorm. And they'd be soaking wet and everybody'd be wet through but you just accepted it. Then we should go with a fork a-piece. You'd pick one sheaf up on your fork and the other chap'd come with his sheaf and we should just stick them together and stack them up as best we could in eights. They were too wet, you see, to pick two up in your arms. Normally you'd pick one up under each arm and bang 'em together.
Barley was the worst, when it was wet, because the barley hames, they stuck all over you. Oh, they were horrible things. They weren't nice at the best of times, when they were dry,

Sheaves stacked up to dry

because some of the hames'd come off and they'd get in your clothes. Barley hames, they only go in one direction, you can't get 'em to come back. They'd work into your clothes. They were horrible prickly things. Barley was a Cinderella crop in my young days. Everybody favoured oats as a cattle feed, whereas nowadays it's all this rolled barley that they go for. They never grow oats for cattle feed much now, horses'll have oats. We never grew a lot of wheat, but we used it for pig feed. Wheat was best for pigs when it was milled up. We didn't put much in cattle feed. At that time oats seemed to be the staple food for our cattle.

I distinctly remember one summer, it was a wet summer and we could <u>not</u> get these sheaves dry. The crows settled on the top of the stacks of wheat sheaves and they trod them down till they were solid, matted lumps of grown corn all in the heads and they were just useless. Lots of the sheaves, we had to cut the strings and open them out to dry. It was going rotten in the middle, the straw was, it was so wet. We had a

terrible summer that year. But at that time, we'd chaps come
and help us, and on a fine drying day, we should cut some of
these sheaves up, spread 'em out to dry. Do as much as we
dare and then, before nightfall, we should gather it all up
loose and cart it home. It'd be stacked up at home and then
we should thresh it as it was, loose, later on. Do the best we
could with it.

There were some bad times as well as good ones then."

There are good memories too. Howard gives a beautifully observed
picture of harvesting by moonlight. This was partly a matter of
necessity, of finishing the job, but it could be quite a romantic time.

"I can remember times when we used to cut, bindering with a
tractor. We should cut all day and then come home and have
a bit of something to eat and me father'd go out to milk and I
should go back into the field, stacking these sheaves up. And
I can remember, many a time I was stacking up in moonlight
till half-past ten – eleven o'clock at night and I <u>really</u> enjoyed
it.

I don't know why, but I can picture meself now in that big
field at the bottom of Stubben Edge, stacking corn up in there,
in a brilliant moon light night, about half past ten at night
and I didn't want to come home. I couldn't believe it now like,
but I was really enjoying it at that time. There was something
nice about it to me. I didn't mind being on my own. I was quite
happy doing this job and doing as much as ever I could before
I had to knock off. You could see ever so plain. When I come
to think of it, the moon was a lot clearer and brighter in those
days. You'd get shadows, but the moon was pretty high in the
sky and it was cooler and quite pleasant work. No
trouble to see your sheaves and stack 'em.

As long as we could see the sheaves it didn't matter.
Properly, you should stack them up with the knot on the outside. Because the sheaf, it's not square across the bottom.
Even when it's a nice straight-standing crop, when the sheaf's
thrown out, the bottom slants. When the binder ties it, it
forms a slope on the butt ends. And you stack that so that it
fits on to the floor properly when it's tapered up at the top.
Ideally, if you can see the knots in the string and put them to
the outside, that's the way it fits. Perhaps, in the moonlight,

we couldn't see the knots but the sheaves had a flat side to them. They weren't totally round. And as you picked 'em up, you could feel and tuck them under your arms and you'd shuffle 'em into shape before you clapped 'em together. You'd get used to it after a while, handling these sheaves. You could feel the proper shape of them. If you got under some big trees somewhere you'd a job to see the sheaves then. But it is lovely, that bright moonlight. I don't know whether there's any truth in the saying – that the harvest moon comes three nights at full moon. It was nice to be actually doing that work. Ah, that type of work, yes. Oh, I shouldn't be going muck-spreading that time of a night, anything like that. No, but this particular job of handling sheaves of corn that's what I seemed to like, to enjoy. Aye. Of course, it wasn't all nice. Some-times you got thistles in amongst it as well and you got prickled and all the inside of your arms got ever so sore, handling sheaves then. Oats weren't too bad because they've nice soft straw, but wheat straw, that was a bit hard on your arms as well. It was hard and tough and that made your arms sore. But somehow we seemed to enjoy it. I don't know why."

The harvested corn was stored in corn stacks outside once the hay-barn was full. The stacks had to be properly built.

"I used to really enjoy that: the corn cutting and stacking these sheaves up and then loading the sheaves on to trailers, carting them home and building the stacks. I really enjoyed pitching these sheaves about. Of course my father, he'd be on the load, putting the sheaves into place on the load and then, when we got home, he'd be stack-building and I should be throwing sheaves up to him. He always used to build these stacks so I never had chance to do that really. That was always his job. But I suppose it was easier than pitching sheaves up to him. I'd got the heavy work, with being younger, I was fitter for it than he was. And so we got on quite nicely that way. But of course we were lucky, we had a hay-barn put up very early on and we just put the sheaves under this hay-barn. We'd no need to bother about roofing it up and thatching it. Till war time came and we grew a lot more corn and we'd more than enough for putting under barn, so we had to build stacks outside. But very often, they'd be threshed at autumn, so they didn't stop long and we should just get by with putting a water proof cover over it till it got threshed out. Then the corn under the barn, that stopped till spring and we threshed that out when fodder were getting shorter again.

There was a real art in building a corn stack. You'd start in the middle at the bottom and keep all the heads off the floor. You wouldn't have the heads on the floor. You'd start with two in the middle, propped up, with the heads sticking up and then you'd start and go round them, keeping the heads in the middle, the sheaves sitting on top of other sheaves all the way. And you'd keep going round and round till you got to the outside of the stack. And then you'd start round the outside, but you always kept the sheaves sloping outwards, so the rain ran out. You'd go a course round the outside and then start and work into the middle again and finish in the middle. And then start another course round the outside and work to the middle again, but always keep the middle filled so that all the sheaves are sloping outwards all the time. And then rain doesn't get in, it runs off. It's quite a skilled job.

Later on, another thing that my father invested in was a Dutch barn. And so we could put our sheaves under this Dutch barn keep it dry, where a lot of the others, they built

All communications to be addressed to—

Telegrams:
" OGLES, RIPLEY, DERBY."   **VICTORIA ROAD.**   Telephone : **92** Ripley.

20/7/31

Folio   **5**   *RIPLEY, Derby,*   193

Mr B Davison   Ashover

Dr. to G. C. OGLE & SONS (Retail) LTD.

Agricultural Engineers & Implement Agents.

5% INTEREST CHARGED
ON OVERDUE ACCOUNTS.   No Receipt valid unless on the Firm's Printed Form.

| June 8 | 1 Dutch Barn (Shire Pattern) 60ft long x 25ft wide x 16/18ft high to eaves with both ends sheeted to eaves level & one side sheeted down 4ft with 24 gauge galvd corugated sheets 22 Gauge Roof Sheets, pitch hole door in each end & with Elevator Fork, rope & pulleys for the sum of :— | £ 115 | 0 | 0 |

Ripley, *12/8/31* 19   **2756**

5

Received *from* Mr B Davison
on account of Ashover
G. C. OGLE & SONS (Retail) Ltd., the
sum of One Hundred and Fifteen Pounds

£ *115 : 0 : 0*   *Per*

stacks outside and they had to thatch them so that was quite a saving."

Before that, the Davisons' stacks were thatched and then stood, protected, until they could be threshed.

"We should save some straw from the previous year, wheat straw to do thatching. When me father was thatching these stacks, it used to be my job, "drawing the thatch". We would tie the bonny rake on to any sort of a frame in the yard – an implement or something upside down. And I'd get this wheat straw and draw it through the teeth of the bonny rake to make it straight and clean. And then put it to one side, ready for thatching. That's what I remember about thatching. I never did any myself because it was always his job."

To make them secure, the thatching was pegged down.

"We had thatch pegs. That was another job. We had to go round and find any small trees, saplings. We cut thatch pegs from them, about two feet long and perhaps as thick as your thumbs, something like that and we would sharpen the end, put a point on one end. And then stick it in the roof and twine some string round it. It would help to hold the thatch down. And these rows of thatch pegs, they'd be perhaps two or three feet apart up the roof of the stack, depending on the length of the straw. You'd have a row of pegs along each layer of straw that he put on.

For the string that we used to use, I spent days tying binder string together. When they were thrashing, they'd cut the string on the sheaves and we asked them to save the strings if they could. They'd let some go through, but they'd save as many as they could. We used to save it and I've spent ages, tying these strings together, to make long lengths, to thatch stacks with. That's how we got by. You could buy what they called thatching band. It was like a thicker, coarser twine and rot-proof. But we used to make do with binder string, because we were pretty economical. We didn't spend a lot of money if we could avoid it."

Thatching was skilful work and care was taken to ensure that the finished result looked perfect. It would take several days to thatch the hay stack.

"Me father'd use some of his wheat straw that he'd thrashed out, to do that. He'd probably have to wait till he'd thrashed at autumn to get this wheat straw. The hay stack'd be covered up with a waterproof sheet until then. And then as soon as he'd got his wheat straw, he'd set to and thatch it."

The combine harvesters saved a lot of this painstaking work.

"Later we got a little combine. It was a six foot wide cut. It cut it and threshed the corn. There was a bagging platform on it and a chap bagged this corn. Then he dropped these bags in heaps in the field and they had to be carried in on a trailer. And it dropped the straw out of the back in little rows. The next combine that I got, that was an eight foot-six cut on that. And again we still bagged the corn on that. At home we used to combine a field, and my father would be bagging on the machine while I was driving it. He'd go home and perhaps start milking and seeing to his cattle. There'd be all these bags of corn in the field and I used to go with a tractor and trailer, I would load these bags myself, hundredweight bags of corn. I'd bring them home and stack these bags. We'd a dryer at that time, it was a big fan and at the outlet we used to stack these bags in a big tunnel in this shed and then close it in at the end. It was tractor-driven, this fan was. We'd start it up and it blew air into this tunnel and it blew it through the bags and it dried the corn that way. And we carried on like that all the time we had this bagging combine. And then stacked the bags in a shed for storage. And then that next combine that I bought, that was a tanker machine. Well that stored the corn on the machine. It was emptied loose into trailers and we brought it back home and then it was augured into the big storage bin that we had. It was stored loose and so that saved a lot more work then. And of course that was dried in the bin. I built a fan on to the base of the bin and it blew air through the bin and dried it that way. And that's still in existence now."

After this period of frantic activity, there was a brief time for relaxation and thanksgiving. But even the harvest celebrations might be tinged with anxious thoughts.

"We never had "Harvest Home". No, we just had the Harvest Festival at Chapel and that was it. Ah. But I know some years we'd not got it in when we had Harvest Festival. They weren't always good summers. I can remember odd times we were still struggling with it when they were singing "All is safely gathered in" and I thought, "That's a bit of a lie!" But we usually managed it, one way or another.

I did enjoy corn harvest. It was a nice time of the year."

THE FARMING YEAR: THRESHING

Once the corn was in, the threshing machine would be ordered and, in time, because it went round all the farms in turn, it would arrive at the farm. Miss Lennox was told that she was "better than the Derbyshire Times" because, as she travelled around she found out exactly where the threshing machine was, so the farmers could work out when it would be coming to them.

What a day that was! Even arranging this could be stressful for the farmer.

"The threshing contractor lived at Westhouses near Alfreton. And we'd got to get in touch with him to come, so, my mate Les decides we'll go on his tandem, him and me together. Now I'd never been on a tandem before. Anyway, we set off and it'd be seven miles at least to Westhouses from our place. And we went and arranged for the threshing tackle and we came back again and of course, I was tired and he wasn't. And he kept going. Oh dear! We got nearer Littlemoor and hills got steeper and Les wouldn't get off, and I couldn't get off! So by the time we got back to Les's place I was about worn out. And I said never again would I ride on a tandem with him. It was the first and last time I've been on that. Oh dear, it nearly killed me!

We always used to have a big threshing session soon after we'd done the harvest, because we should be wanting some fodder for winter cattle. And then, during the winter we'd use that fodder up and come February, March time there was a second threshing do and that'd last us through till the next autumn again."

Threshing machinery was usually hired from a contractor. In
Ashover it was organised communally. The Ashover Threshing
Company Limited bought its own threshing machine and the
members could use it, taking turns. Miss Bassett explains:

"This was a travelling machine with a steam engine which it
took it round to different farms. They made me Secretary and
the farmers all round about could each have £5 worth of
shares. They bought their own machine anyway, the farmers
did and I did all the accounts for them. It was run as a
proper company and we paid dividends every year. I had to
collect all the money from the different farms, and then it
paid a dividend, 25 shillings. We had meetings every month
in the autumn and springtime and then it lay dormant until
the next autumn, until the next lot of harvest came in. Oh, it
was a very flourishing little company at first, well it was until
the combine came in and the threshing machines weren't
needed anymore."

"When the time came to have this corn thrashed out,"
continues Howard, " in those days it was the old steam engine
that came with a threshing drum and a chopper and a tie-er
hung on the back of it. They'd come down our lane into the
stack yard and it was a major job, setting the threshing drum
up, because it had to be level, so it had to be jacked up and
wooden packings put under the wheels. The old steamers,
they were big lumbering things, and we always used to have
to get a ton of coal in for a steam engine to thresh for us for a
day and carry water to it as well, because it used no end of
water. To get over carrying water, we ran a hose pipe from the
tap in the yard and filled it up with that. So that did away
with carrying water."

The threshing machine had to be constantly supplied with coal and
water. The machines used a lot of water as Bert Hopkinson
remembers:

"There were two water troughs down Mill Lane, fed by a
spring which never went dry. The farms at Woolley carted
water from it on threshing days to keep the steam traction
engines at work."

The whole farming community was involved, says Howard.

"Every farmer had to have about a dozen men, to help thresh and do all the jobs. We'd have ten or twelve, and then it'd be my turn to go round to these other neighbouring farmers to help them. But I never went into Woolley and I never went into Ashover. It all centred round Milltown and Littlemoor area. And that's how we seemed to carry on. We seemed to get enough men from just our locality to do the job. There'd be two on the stack putting sheaves on to the threshing drum, there'd be two on the threshing drum, one cutting strings and the other one feeding the drum. There'd be two chaps carrying corn. There'd be one chap on the chopping machine feeding the chopper if you were chopping, there'd be one carrying the chop. There'd be another one emptying the chop in the shed, or if they were tying the straw there'd be one looking after the tie-er and another chap carrying the bundles away and another one on the stack building it. So there were a lot of men to see to."

Millie Ablett recalls:

"We hired the thrashing drum – Bradley's from Alton. We had to wait our turn. The farmers used to go from farm to farm helping each other out. We ground it up for the cows. We just grew enough for ourselves. If there was an exceptionally good crop, they'd probably sow some back into ground when it was time for drilling again."

A gang of men would follow the itinerant threshing machines. Olive Scott explains.

Ashover Threshing Co., Ltd.

.... 192_

Mr. _____

			£	s.	d.
Threshing	....	....	2	0	0
Chopping	....	....		15	0
Tieing	....	....			
			2	15	0

"There used to be these men – we used to call them roadsters
– they used to go to farms year after year when it were
threshing day. And I remember me Dad saying that one of
these chaps said to him, "When we go to a place we always
look at cats and at dog" he says, "and we know whether we're
going to get aught to eat." And then they'd move on from place
to place, follow on. Oh yes. Walter used to go down there, and
me father did, to help when they were thrashing. It were a
marvellous contraption. You could hear it chugging away."

Besides the threshing gangs the local men and farmers depended
on each other and worked together. Walter Hopkinson would help
on
"All the farms round about. Joe Marriot's and Ken
Wheatcrofts', Jack Hardwick and people like that, and at
Knotcross. Everybody would help all together."

Ernest Purdy was the band-cutter, on top of the threshing
machine, Walter recalls.
"He cut the bands and then it went through the machine and
there were men either taking the straw or the corn away or
something like that."

"It was my mother's job to feed them every day" Howard
continues. "And I don't know how she coped with it because,
with 11 or 12 hungry chaps coming in at dinner-time, there was
some food shifted. And then there'd be tea-time as well, because
they all used to have their tea. So it was an awful busy time for
everybody. And then of course, the threshing machine 'd move
out to the next farm – they'd want me to go and help them. So
everybody was going round one farm or another, threshing for
people. That's how we got the men to help us. I used to have
days and days going round other farms locally, threshing and I
seemed to enjoy it at that time, but it was a dirty, dusty job."

The men would come into the house for their main meal, as
Margaret Graney remembers. Her mother would cook enormous
meals for the men with Margaret helping. There were some huge
plates that were kept in the cellar and only brought out at
threshing time.

Threshing gets underway at Lydgate Farm Wingerworth.

Millie Ablett describes the tremendous amount of work involved.
    "Of course you fed the men. And if it was raining, and they
    couldn't do the thrashing, you'd got all the food ready and
    you'd no fridges. You'd got probably a cellar head or cold
    pantry. Because it was good food. And you'd always got to
    have a pudding. And then drinks during the day to wash the
    dust down."

Hilda Hopkinson remembers that
    "At threshing time, the farmer's wife would have us in,
    peeling all these potatoes, because they must have a good
    lunch, the workmen as came with the threshing machine. It
    took us ages to peel these potatoes. I think they must have
    boiled them in the copper because there were such a lot. I can
    remember doing that at Brailsfords and at Tinkley Lane
    Farm."

"In some places," Howard recalls, "the farmers'd let water get
into the stacks and oh, they were in a terrible mess, some of
them. They'd gone fusty and they were really unhealthy. This

white mould pothers about, a white dust, when you shift it. And the sheaves would be solid, grown together, because the rain had been going through these stacks. They'd built them wrong altogether. I mean a good stack-builder wouldn't get rain into a stack at all. They always used to say, "keep your middle well filled in" so that the sheaves are sloping outwards and then it shelves the rain out. But some of these farmers, they didn't do that. The middle was hollow and water 'd run in from the sides and from the roof and oh! they were a mess, particularly if they'd stopped till spring. There was hardly a good sheaf left in the whole stack. They were terrible jobs then. Well, they were hardly worth threshing. I mean, it wasn't palatable stuff, even the grain was poor quality. I don't know how they managed, the poor cattle. They must have had to eat all sorts of rubbish. But I know we never had that. Me father'd have gone mad if he'd a wet sheaf anywhere in a stack. It didn't suit him at all and it didn't me either. No, I like to have things good.

If it was wheat we were threshing first, my father always had the straw chopped up and that served for cattle feed. It was mixed with mangolds and turnips that were pulped up. They were mixed up in a big heap and fed to the cattle in the winter. And so the first thing was to get this chopper hung on to the back of the threshing drum. The straw came out of the threshing drum, dropped into this chopper, and there was a chap feeding the straw. It chopped it all up into short bits and then it was bagged and another fellow carried the bags of chop into the chamber. The bags were what they call four bushel bags. That's what they used to have in early days. They were railway sacks; real thick hessian – ever such thick strong bags they were. And they used to hump these 18 stone bags about, they were stronger men than they are now."

These bags were used for various crops. They were filled by volume and the weight would vary according to the contents. In some instances they would carry these bags up into a chamber on the farm, if they were keeping the corn.

"But they might have a sack lifter there that wound the sacks up to shoulder height. Then the chap'd pull it across his shoulders, and carry in into a chamber. But it was still hard going. I could never carry an 18 stone bag. I could happen manage 14 at most, but it was hard going for me. Usually 10, 12 stones at best, to carry into chamber. There was another fellow in the chamber emptying these bags and treading the chop down so that it didn't bulk up too much. It was quite a laborious job that, dusty, dirty job as well. And when we'd chopped the wheat straw, it was the oat straw then to cope with and that was tied up in bundles. So the chopping machine was pulled out of the way and the tie-er was drawn up to the back of the threshing drum and the straw dropped into that; and as it dropped in it was bundled and tied up with two strings, and there was a chap carried these bundles away to where another fellow was building the straw stack and of course that was built up. And we fed the oat straw for cattle to eat, like hay. It was quite good food for them, we put it in the manger. And then anything that was left, it was just used for bedding, we got rid of that in that way.

The machine that tied these bundles was similar to a

This picture shows a belt driven machine powered by the tractor on the left. The grain is being gathered into sacks and the straw would come out, tied, on the other side.

binder. It had fingers that packed the straw down and when
the bundle got to a certain size, it tripped a lever and the
needles came up and tied string round it, two strings, to hold
it together because it was so long. The straw that used to
come out of the tie-er at the back of the threshing drum, we
used to call that bottles of straw, not sheaves any more after
it had been threshed. They were bigger – because the tie-er
would pack it in longer pieces and bigger diameter- it spread
itself out more. The threshing drum is four feet six wide and
the straw'd come out almost that width so your bottle of
straw'd be four foot long. And then we should put it in a stack
and that'd be used either for feed or bedding. Sometimes
they'd have an elevator at the stack, to take it up, if it was a
big stack, but we never had that, we used to just pitch it up
with a fork, and that's the only way we did it, because the
modern balers that we know, they weren't used.

There was the big stationary baler and it made big, solid,
very heavy bales and early on they were tied with wire. There
was one chap looking after this baler and he threaded this
wire through needles and it came round through the two ends
together and just twisted them to hold them together. They
were big heavy bales, they'd be at least a hundred weight in
each of them and you'd carry them on your back to the stack.
I've had some sore backs with that job. And then later on, it
got to string tying. It'd still got to have a chap there to use
these needles to thread the string round the bale, but it was
kinder stuff than wire. Wire, it was terrible. You couldn't get
your fingers under it or anything. It was too tight. And of
course, there was the danger of wire in cattle feed, if bits
broke off it or rusted. It was too dangerous, so they
eventually went on to string tying and there was a lot of that
done – big balers. But we never had that done. It was either
tied or chopped.

And the chaff, that usually came out, off the riddles, underneath at the end. And we should have one chap there,
carrying that chaff into a chamber, for bedding during the
winter, to bed cows down with. Sometimes, they'd have what
they called a chaff blower on it and that'd blow the chaff into
a big heap away from drum and then they might burn it, if
they didn't need to use it. These big arable farms in

Lincolnshire that's what they did there, but we always used to save it because it was useful for bedding.

Aye I can remember helping other folks to go thrashing and very often, it was my job carrying straw bales. I'd got the heavy end because I was daft enough to take the heavy job. I used to struggle with these big bales all day. It was a tiring job and me back'd be red-raw at the end of the day because we should sweat with the work and it was most uncomfortable.

I used to like to get on the stack. That was my favourite place, pitching sheaves from the stack on to drum. Because there was an art in that really. I've watched some chaps on the stack, they'd keep throwing sheaves up on to the drum, piling them up, faster than the band cutter could get rid of them. And they'd get a great heap and the poor fellow on the drum, he couldn't sort 'em out, they'd be fast under one another. And I've known the time when he's shoved the lot off onto the floor again with his hands and told 'em to start again. But I always used to, if I could, feed the sheaves up all the same way, heads first, on to the side of the drum on to the board where the band cutter was and as he took one off I put another there. And I used to try and keep that going nice and steady and you got on a lot faster that way. Sometimes I should put two up. I should wait till he'd shifted two and then put two more up. I should be able to get one sheaf on one grain of the fork and one on the other grain of the fork side be side and put 'em up as they lay flat, heads together on the side of the drum and then the band cutter, he'd just pick these two up in turn and as he shifted the last one, I should put another couple on. I used to pride myself on doing that job and we used to get on ever so well. Because, very often there'd be two of us on the stack and I should have somebody throwing sheaves to me to put on the drum. We shouldn't both be pitching on to the drum. He'd leave that to me and the other chap 'd be on the other side of the stack, because it'd be a big stack and to save me walking about, fetching them, he'd be feeding me and then I should throw 'em up on to the drum. Aye. That was my favourite job."

They were extraordinarily busy days. Olive's dad:

"Took my little dog when Mr Davison was threshing. 'Cause

he was a Bedlington Terrier and he were a good ratter. I
forgot how many rats he chopped. Because of course the rats
scoot everywhere, on a day like that. They could do wi' Pied
Piper there I should think."

Another method of dealing with rats was to "stick 'em with their
pitchforks" as Margaret Graney recalls. Millie Ablett remembers
that
"They would have a piece of wire netting round where they
were working to stop the rats. There'd be somebody with a
dog, little Jack Russell dog; it would have a whale of a time."

It was not just rats that might cause a problem. Mrs Butler
remembers one threshing time in particular:
"I had a friend here with me. And Roy Burdett brought a
little sweet bag and he passed it over. Inside there were little
baby pink mice, they'd got them out of the corn stack of
course. We were silly shrieky girls and we did some shrieking
and squawking."

"And that's how we carried on all through war-time." Howard
concludes. "Gradually we grew more corn and then the old
steam threshing engine was redundant because bigger
tractors came in. They imported a lot from America at that
time, on lease-lend as they called it, and these threshing
contractors, they bought a big strong tractor to do the
threshing for us, so that made it a bit more convenient.
Later on, combining came in and that did away with
threshing and baling straw and the whole system of farming
changed quite quickly then."

THE FARMING YEAR:
THE FODDER AND ROOT CROP HARVEST

"In the cycle of the year the next thing, after we'd got the corn
harvest in, we'd got to start thinking about planting winter
wheat. So you'd start ploughing again. It was the same
procedure, work it down with harrows and sow your wheat on
it and harrow it in and leave that to grow.

Meanwhile there were other crops to harvest, lints for example, which is vetches, like peas and lentils. It was cattle feed. We used to mow it and cart it in for the cattle. The chap who used to work on our farm, he'd go, with a horse and cart, into this patch of lints and mow so much, with a scythe, and load it into this cart and take it home and feed it to the cows. They ate it as it was. It was all tangled up stuff. You can imagine, peas would be. They all grow together and it was a bit of a job separating it out. But we did jobs like that in that time. You separated it with a scythe to mow. I don't know whether they fed it inside, or threw it out in the field for them. It'd be in forkfuls. I remember (I was only a little kid at the time) riding in the cart. I should ride with the chap, and sit and watch him do the job and ride back again. I don't think we grew it for long. I suppose me father'd think it wasn't worth all the trouble of growing it. It'd be early 1930's when we were doing that. As soon as war broke out things changed drastically. Crop growing, it speeded up a lot. It had to or else we should have starved."

The first of the root crops to be lifted were the potatoes. All this work, until tractors were used, needed a lot of men.

"For the hoeing and weeding in turnips and mangolds and that, you'd perhaps have three or four people you'd ask to come and help. And then potato picking, that was another job. Sometimes you used to get school children to do that. But perhaps in earlier years there were grown-up people who'd come in and help to do it. Labour was easily obtained then, and cheap and you could afford to have people to help you. We hadn't a potato spinner at that time, but we'd a gadget on a plough that lifted the potatoes out and brought them to the surface, with a lot of soil of course, and then we had to pick 'em all by hand and forage about among the soil to get them that way. But it was still a messy job and eventually we had a potato spinner. That made a better job of it, cleaned them out and it was easier picking, but it were still a laborious work. It was a bit crude but the next best thing to forking the potatoes out.

Often children would be employed to help with this, especially during the war years. Joe Holmes remembers:

"We used to have that fortnight off school in October, we used
to call it tater picking holiday. We all used to go tater picking.
There's none o' that now. Ah, a lot of 'em were picked by
children. All farmers got taters. They'd all got these little
spinners. They used to spin 'em out. But you had to pick 'em
all up. We all used to go when I were going to school, tater
picking for somebody. Ah, we used to get a bit of pocket money
and a few taters to take home wi' you. I used to go to Unwins,
where Tommy Outram lived. He had one or two tater fields on
the roadside, there was one down at the bottom, Miners' end,
and then that one opposite Post Office, that long field. We'd
take a few sandwiches. We didn't used to bother with hot
drinks, if you could get a drink of water, it'd be all right. If it
were a wet week we didn't used to bother then. They couldn't
get 'em out then. Used to go Saturdays then, till we got 'em
done. Saturdays and Sundays happen, if we got good
weather. Till we got 'em out."

There were mangolds for winter feed for the cattle. These were
harvested before the turnips because they were easily damaged by
frost. Howard continues:

"We'd them to pull, clean and top and cart off and tip into a
big heap in the stack. The pulling and the cutting, that was
all done by hand. It was a slow miserable job, particularly
when it was frosty, wet, we had some nasty days to work in.
We had what was called a turnip knife and it was like a blade,
about 12 inches long with a handle on the end of it, and quite
a strongish blade. In fact, sometimes we used to use old
scythe blades. Cut the end off a scythe blade and stick a
handle on it and some people used to use them for cleaning
and topping mangolds. But in a way they were too sharp, thin
blades and you'd damage the mangold too much. The proper
turnip knife was thicker and more controllable. But it was
still a slow, back-aching job. And then we came with a horse
and cart again and loaded them up and carted them into the
stack yard, shot 'em up in a big heap and they were covered
up with straw first and then with soil, to keep the frost off.
But sometimes we shouldn't perhaps have time to cart them
up that night and any that were left, if it was going to freeze

Howard Davidson on his 78th brithday.

Wren.

March 14TH 1986.

The Wren painted by Ted Hellaby,

Ploughing with a single furrow horse-drawn plough at Farley.

A steady team pose for the camera.

A cottager's pig.

Brown Leghorns.

June 11ᵗʰ 1986.

Buff. Leghorns.

The Hellaby farm poultry.

Feb. 23rd 1976.

Springtime

Ted Hellaby's lambs.

Sheep dipping with a portable dip at Hilltop Farm, Ashover. 1928.

Wild roses painted by Ted Hellaby.

Turning the hay to dry it with the swath-turner. Bernard Davison at Dale Bank Farm.

The last forkful of hay goes onto the load.

Dec 31ST 1972.

Badgers painted by Ted Hellaby.

Opening out for cutting corn at Hilltop Farm.

Harvesting with a self-binder at Hilltop Farm, Ashover in 1932.

October 5th. 1975.

Horned cattle painted by Ted Hellaby.

Arthur Hind designed his own milk advertisement.

Ted Hellaby's portrait of an Ayrshire heifer.

A traction engine and threshing machine in action.

Oct 16TH 1977.

Ted Hellaby's bull.

October 5TH 1977.

Loading at evening time. Ted Hellaby evokes the peace at the end of the day's work.

One of the Bassetts' Blue Albion herd on show at Ashover.

A selection of Arthur Hind's prize cards from local ploughing matches.

The Greyhound Inn, Milltown, showing the cowsheds on the right.

The Hellabys' decorative light turnout at Ashover Show.

June 29th 1986.

Ted Hellaby records the light turnout in his own style.

Grazing Kale.
Oct. 9th 1976

Cattle grazing kale painted by Ted Hellaby.

that night, we used to have to cover them up with the tops to stop the frost getting at 'em. Otherwise, they went rotten. And then the next day we should uncover them again and try and get them carted off."

And in between times, when necessary, there was kale to cut. With its leaves laden with icy water this could be a most unpleasant job. Another cold job was turnip pulling.

"Aye," Joe says, laconically, "You could go chopping turnips if you wanted. That was a cold job in winter time, cold for your fingers. Things have changed. Farmers used to grow a lot of turnips and that sort of thing for beasts in them days. They don't much now. It were all turnips and mangolds then. Every farm had so many mangolds on it. You were paid by the time you did, by the hour."

But, as Miss Bassett muses,

"They don't grow turnips and they don't feed turnips now. It's all concentrated cakes and nuts and things. Cattle are like the human being. They prefer fresh things than the old fashioned dishes I think."

Joe Holmes echoes this:

"There's no turnip pulling now, is there? Ah, they used to pull 'em by hand. Take tops off and chop bottom. Chuck 'em into a row, then they'd come and pick 'em up after."

Miss Bassett describes this onerous work.

"I used to be able to use a little hand sickle thing. And that was because we used to grow fields of turnips in those days, to feed cattle with in the winter. And they were gathered by hand. You had a sickle and you pulled out the turnip and knocked the top off and went down the row. It was an endless job, turnip growing and they have to be weeded and – oh it was a horrid, I won't say horrid, but an endless job – from spring right up until the autumn time when they were gathered in."

Turnip pulling could be a hazardous job. Millie Ablett has

"One or two scars to prove mangold and turnip pulling. You

used to walk up the row and you'd got quite a big knife, a proper tool. You'd pull up the turnip; trim the root and then woof! you'd throw them into the cart. "Go on, gee up" – that was when horse knew when to go. "Whoa!" and it'd stop. That was quite a long process, because we grew quite a few. And then they were all stacked up in big heaps when you got home."

Joe Holmes explains further,
"You'd take 'em in the stack yard and cover 'em up, with straw so frost wouldn't get at 'em. They was no good in winter, if frost had been at 'em. Then they used to have to have a machine for pulping 'em before they give 'em to beasts. They didn't give 'em to cows whole. They used to have to pulp 'em.

"When I were on spar job," Joe continues, "When I was at Conways, I used to take a bag of mangolds every year to an old farmer's wife at Bradwell, so she could make jam. She used to say, "Bring me my mangolds Joe, when they're ready." I used to get 'em from old Joe Bradley at Handley. She used to make mangold jam. I'd never heard of it before."

Also, Margaret Graney recalls,
"You could buy brewery grains – the fermented grain which had been used in making beer. When delivered, they would still be warm, with steam coming off them. They were put into a pit and you had to tread them down to stop the air getting to them or they would have gone mouldy. You cut them with a hay knife and mixed them with turnips to feed the cows. You had to be careful not to mix in too much grains or your cows would be wobbling around!"

Ted Hellaby's diary:
  21 March 1931 " Fetched two loads of grain from Stretton"
  30 July 1931 " Trod grains this morning."

Once the roots were harvested, the ploughing, which had begun with the end of the corn harvest could be completed. It is the close of a cycle, but not an end, for the work of ploughing joins the end of the year and its beginning.

THE FARMING YEAR: SEASONAL JOBS

There were seasonal jobs too, Howard points out.

"One thing about farming, it was a varied life. New jobs were always coming up. You didn't have one job that got monotonous over a year. You'd a variety of jobs and there was always a change coming ahead for you. If it was a nasty job, it didn't last for ever and you got on to something else."

If wet weather interrupted work, there was an opportunity to get other jobs done.

"Of course, in summer we had to white-wash all the cowsheds out. We'd clean all the cobwebs down and scrape all the muck off the walls. And then we'd a white-washing machine and we used to mix this quick lime up in an old tub and spray it on cow shed walls. Make it all clean and sweet smelling again for a while. That was usually a wet day job in summer."

John Heathcote remembers one occasional job he really enjoyed.

"I've done a lot of walling, I have that. Up on tops it were all walls. It's a marvellous job if you get interested. Odd times there'd be walls come down and they'd need repairing. Odd times wind'd fetch 'em down, if there were a bad wind. Sometimes you'd have poachers going round after rabbits. Very often rabbits go in bottom of wall, and they had dogs as would run down side of wall, and they'd tell you if there were a rabbit in the wall. They'd stick their nose in. And what happened, if folks went after rabbit, they'd pull two stones out and get rabbit out, and that went but there were a hole left in wall, and it weren't long afore wall started coming down. It happened, it did.

If you're walling and you've nowt to think about, you can just go and set to and – it's a really interesting job, walling. Me grandfather taught us how to wall build and – what he always said was "You don't pick a stone up and put it down again. You put it on t'wall." Some people, you see, will pick a stone up and measure it up and if it don't fit they'll put it down and find another bit. He didn't. He said there's a place for 'em all on t'wall if you find it. He were right and all. He'd come and show you. Do it like this. And then he'd gone. But he'd expect you to do it like he'd shown you. Oh yes. It all comes to you pretty naturally, them sort of jobs. If you're interested you can do it."

Christmas time made extra work, as another farmer remembers. "When it came near Christmas time you would come up the yard from milking and smell burning chickens' feet and feathers. In the fire in the kitchen range you'd see the feet and legs. Chicken feathers – and fleas – would be floating around the kitchen. About 50 birds would be killed each year. Mother would singe off the soft under-feathers by holding the bird over newspaper that she had set fire to on the hearth. They would send one of these birds, (they were mostly cockerels), to relatives. It would go, wrapped in greaseproof paper, into a cardboard box. The bits and bobs of giblets and some correspondence would be put in with it and the spaces filled with newspapers. Brown paper (the inner lining of a feed bag) and string was used to wrap the box and sealing wax, melted with a candle, would be dribbled on. It was then taken to the Post Office where the Post Mistress would look at it rather disparagingly over the top of her glasses before she dealt with it."

There was a roaring trade in chickens at Christmas time. "Nearing Christmas a fellow from Kelstedge would go round the farms, buying young cockerels to sell. He would put them on his cart and fasten them with a net." Olive was amused to hear that "This particular farmer, knowing he hadn't got any cockerels, saw one or two appear in his yard. He said, "If you can find any you can have them." The chap grabbed them, put them on his cart and one or two more appeared. At last, having paid the farmer for several cockerels, the fellow realised that his netting was broken and that as he put a couple of birds on his cart, one or two others were escaping. The farmer did quite well out of it."

MECHANISATION AND WARTIME

It was useful to have someone who was mechanically minded, for the days of working with horses were going by the time Howard started working.

"My father always did the horses and I was only 14 when we first had a tractor. Of course I was all into machinery at my age then and I let me father keep the horses. I grew up on the tractor. Me father wasn't bothered about the tractor much. See, he was a horse man all the time and he enjoyed his horses and so he was quite content for me to take over any mechanical things and we managed quite well like that. For years after we had a tractor we still kept a horse to do light work, turnip drilling and rolling and chain harrowing, things like that. But horses were going out fast. As soon as the war broke out everybody seemed to get on to tractors and the horses, they disappeared early on during the war. They didn't seem to last long after the tractors came into work.

The little tractor was about 25 horse-power, and they were considered quite powerful machines in those days. That one cost £330. Aye. That's all. That was in 1940. And then, the one that I bought in 1957, that was 32 horse-power. That was really good. And of course nowadays, they think nothing of 100,150 horse power. But that's how times have changed.

We bought the first one in 1940 and we used it for two years. And then, something went wrong with the engine. We took it into Kennings at Clay Cross, where we had bought it from, and they found out that an oil gallery had never been drilled through completely and part of the engine wasn't getting any oil. And it had run dry all that time. And so, they said they'd do the engine up and make it good, but we decided we'd have a new tractor instead, in 1942. Because

that first tractor, it hadn't any hydraulic lift on the back for putting a plough and cultivator on. So we had this other new one with a hydraulic lift on it, made it better. And then, I think plough cost £50 and the cultivator was £50. It was nothing, was it? I mean, we could afford to buy new things like that in those days. But we couldn't now. The price of new tackle now is well beyond our reach. We seemed to be able to afford to buy things like that then, new implements to do the work with it. A mowing machine, you see, before we had a tractor, it was all horse-drawn tackle and that didn't fit very well with a tractor, so we had to buy a mowing machine and hay loader and side-rake and things like that, to do the work with. But we could afford to do it in those days.

We had a tedder early on and I think we did adapt that for pulling with a tractor. The tines folded up and you pulled 'em out – they were spring-loaded, you pulled 'em out till they were sticking straight out across a wooden bar. And it went

round and picked up grass up and flung it out at the back. We
didn't work all night like they do now. My oldest tractor never
had lights for a long time. And then I rigged it up with one
light. But I never did any night work with it, it was just a
novelty at that time. I don't think we ever used it, not for
working in the fields."

Equipment and tools had to be maintained.

"We bought the mowing machine in 1939. When the little
treads on the wheels got worn away – (of course, doing road
work didn't help it) they got till they were nearly smooth and
what I did then: I got two tyres from the old trailer muck-
spreader that we used to have, (it had treaded wheels, like
miniature tractor wheels, with tread bars on them) and I cut
the treaded part off and bolted it on to the arms and brought
it back to life again.

We used to have a grindstone on two stone posts set in
ground. Axle rested on top of the stone posts in little steel
bearings. We'd use it to sharpen cutting knives and bill hooks
and brushing hooks and anything like that. A brushing hook
was long-handled, with a curved blade on the end, that you
cut hedges with."

And sometimes work could be done for other people.

"After I got me decent workshop, there's been some weird and wonderful things gone out of that place that I've made for folks. I remember once making a bullpen for a chap. A big, strong, tubular bullpen. And when I'd finished it, I suddenly realised, am I going to get it out? And it'd only just go out through doors, it was that big. When I'd finished welding it together, I thought, 'Have I got to start and cut it to pieces again, to get it out?' And there was another trailer, a big long bale trailer I made for a chap. And we left the drawbar off till we'd finished everything else, because when I put the draw-bar on, we couldn't shut the doors. It were too long, it was sticking outside. So we had to wait and make a big effort one day, to get this drawbar on and get it out, so that I could shut me doors and lock 'em. Ah, that was when things got bigger and bigger. And of course, nowadays, you can't get a tractor in me workshop. They're too big, too high. They won't go under my doors at all. So I don't get many repairs now, but anything that is in need, I've got to do it outside."

The war was the catalyst.

"Admitted, it was wartime and we were getting better prices for everything that we produced. That seemed to set things going better. We used to have a little stationary engine for driving the corn mill for grinding the corn. And then, it was a slow job, it was only a little tiny mill. So we decided we'd buy a bigger mill and then we thought we should have to drive it with a tractor, so, we bought a pulley to fit on the back of the tractor. And that was only £12 10s for a pulley, to fit on the tractor. You wouldn't buy the bolts for it now, for that money. And I've still got them all now, still got the pulley and the tractor.

As soon as war came out, everything changed and they paid us well to produce as much food as we possibly could. So it put everybody on their feet and it was a real good time for farmers during the war. We could afford to buy machinery and employ labour and we got on ever so well. And in my case, I went out contracting as well with a tractor and it really made a nice sideline for me, as well as farming at home. I got quite a bit of money to myself as well, during the war years, through working hard that way. I know it was long hours and hard work really but I enjoyed it when I was young. Of course, during that time, me father could afford to pay a man to help him on the farm while I was out contracting. I just did nothing but tractor work at home and away and they saw to the cattle at home. And we got on very well that way.

The only thing that you could say were contractors in times previous were the threshing chaps – they were going round to all the farms doing their threshing for them and they'd be the contractor in that business.

I'd not go very far really. Just Ashover, Woolley, Stretton and top of Butterley up here. That's about as far as I ever went round. But there were no end of little farms, it wasn't economical for them to have tractors and do their own work. And so I went and did their little bit. Perhaps only ploughed a couple of fields for them and drilled it for them and then we'd cut the corn for them and sometimes they'd even feed the sheaves, just as they were, to the cattle. They wouldn't have it threshed. They'd just milk a few cows and make one churn of milk. That's how they used to carry on in a little way.

War-time, in a way was a good thing for the farmers. It made us wanted and we could sell good stuff and we were earning a decent living out of it. Because up till then, farming, it was a very dead end job. There were not much profit out of it. Farmers couldn't afford to buy tractors or anything."

For the first few years
"People engaged in agriculture were exempt from war duties and there were quite a few people wanted you to take them on, to get them out of going to fighting. And we had chaps like that all during the war, coming helping us. On our pay-roll more or less, to keep them out of going to war. And I was exempt, on this farming job."

John Heathcote discovered that he too was exempt.
"Yes. I remember going to sign on and when he asked what I were doing I said well, farming like. He said had I any preference for what I were going into and I said Army and he said I don't think you'll need to bother. You'd better get off

back home again. There were three of us off same farm and we all got same thing."

"There was no targets," continues Howard, "but grow as much as you could. And if you made a good effort and showed willing, they appreciated you. But some farmers were slip-shod and negligent and then they did get on to them and make them stir themselves up a bit and produce something. Because it was a desperate time. We were starving. They wanted every crumb that they could get out of our own farmers and as long as you made a good effort, you were really appreciated. It's true that the inspectors did come round to have a look at your crops and see they was growing all right but if you were all right, well, you got a bit of praise and that was it and they left you alone."

Much land that had been lying idle was brought into use, John explains.

"There were plenty work to do while war were on. We were producing food. Like I said, before war there wasn't a lot of arable land but then when war were on, they started and they ploughed everywhere up to grow corn, to grow oats and wheat and barley and that sort of thing."

They were still basically dairy farms but "You were bringing more ground into use. Such a lot of ground, in them days, that had never been ploughed up. Best thing that ever happened to it really, when they ploughed it up."

Even permanent grassland, the grazing land, was to be used for food crops.

MINISTRY OF AGRICULTURE AND FISHERIES.

Regd. No. H.D.

Date

(Voucher No.)

Inspection of Growing Crops of Potatoes.

FEE PAYABLE :—

For inspection of / acres.

Entered by

Fee Book No.

Total

RECEIVED

15-AUG 1932

FOR CASHIER, MINISTRY OF AGRICULTURE & FISHERIES

Form No. 687/H.D.

THIS ACKNOWLEDGMENT SHOULD BE RETAINED.

MINISTRY OF AGRICULTURE AND FISHERIES,
MINISTRY OF AGRICULTURE AND FISHERIES,
80, LEONARD STREET,
HOTEL MAJESTIC, LONDON, E.C.2.

ST. ANNES (Date of mark.)

LANCS.

The receipt is hereby acknowledged of your letter of the *application* stating that you propose to plough up permanent grassland in your occupation.

Form No. 410/S.S.

*50m 5/39—[7696] 81521/1042 100m 10/39 G & S 704/9

The war did mean though that there were changes on the farm. John Hodgson explains.

"During the last part of the war, the Ministry took over different farms. And they took over Gladwin's Mark. It was an experimental farm. But it was general farming and they showed you different management of land and crop dressing, root crops, self-sufficiency. And from there, I was transferred down to the machinery depot in Chesterfield and that was all tractor work – you went out on to these marginal schemes – hillside farms, re-seeding."

It seems that it was possible for an inefficient farmer to turn the tables!

"One farmer round here, he was a rotten poor farmer, and what made everybody so mad: he got a job on the War Ag. committee. He packed up farming and got a job working for them. And when he came on the scene, everybody could have shot him. They were disgusted with him! I don't know what eventually happened, I think that they perhaps shifted him to another area, where he wasn't known. I remember that ever so well."

Wartime brought potential danger to a peaceful occupation. Tom

Limb, who at the age of 17 enlisted into the RAF, describes one incident:

"One summer during the war the people who rented the field next to our cottage had turned it over to hay. They were mowing it. My mother and father went in the hayfield to help. The wife was on the top of the haycart, her husband's on the tractor and my parents are handing up hay on a fork. A plane came over, very low, and the wife waved to it, saying to my mother, "There's your Tom there!" She's waving away and all of a sudden, her husband jumps off the tractor. "Get under the wall, it's a German!" He'd seen the markings on it. My parents jumped under the wall with him. His wife's still waving away and it went off over Littlemoor."

Even soldiers in training might face unexpected danger, as he goes on to explain

"I came home on leave. I was going to see this girl who lived above Critchlows. There were six fields on the back. George and Mary were breeding young bullocks for the beef market. They knocked the walls down so the beasts could wander. They'd got about 30 young bullocks. I was just going through the stile up to this girl's home when I saw George and I was talking to him. He'd reared his head up over the wall. He was wearing a trilby hat and a sack bagging for a cloak over his shoulders. Just then, three army lorries drew up just above the road from Matlock. All these soldiers jumped out with a young officer with walking-stick and pipe, and they went up Critchlow's field on manoeuvres. I said,

"Oh, you can't stop 'em George. They're on manoeuvres, they can go anywhere." He says, "They'll be manoeuvring in a bit."

All at once, all these bullocks came after them. And they're running down the field, the officer leading. They all jumped over the wall into the road. And George and I are laughing, so this young officer said,

"Are they your cattle?"

"Ah" he says, "they dunno take kindly to khaki."

He says, "Before this war is over, you'll thank God in heaven for the British Army." George says, "I knows that, thou knows that. Try telling them buggers that."

At Williamthorpe the war did not affect Colin Marriott's life too much.

"We had some good times and bad 'uns. Suppose we were lucky just round about here, with bombs. They went over, but they only dropped a few loads round about. We did have one at Holmewood, not far from farm where Georgie lived, in one of their fields there. I always remember being sat in pictures one night when they went off. I thought the picture place would come down. Then one dropped at Stainsby, we heard that rattling. Then they had one at Duckmanton, near school. We didn't have many. Funnily enough, there were Grassmoor Works not far away. They were making coke, petrol and all sorts. It was a big place, that. And then that one at Holmewood that were making coke and petrol. My mate and my cousin used to work where they made petrol there. And they were never damaged. We had some lucky escapes.

If they landed in a field, there'd be a great big hole to fill in. That's what happened at Holmewood. Massive great big hole. Two lads that lived at Holmewood Farm were watching this aeroplane flying round, right over farm and they could tell it were Gerry and then next thing, couldn't understand why he didn't drop 'em on place. He either didn't want to, or didn't aim very good, because he dropped 'em all round pit. There weren't one landed on factory. And it was a lovely moonlight night (they wouldn't come if there wasn't any moonlight, because they couldn't see). No, it didn't half put wind up the two lads. They were standing in farm yard, and it blew glass out of windows, took great big doors off barn at back. I don't think they ever came up Woodthorpe way, though. I never heard of any damage up this road.

I were down at Chesterfield one day and siren went. It were going dark. I were with this girl, we'd arranged to meet me brother. Two of his mates were going back into Forces. And they stopped to get some drink and I didn't go, and I said "Well, I'll pick you up at such a time" and by gum, air-raid siren started to go. So anyway, we went down and we couldn't find 'em, and warden said "You've got to go, you can't stop here". So he cleared us off and we come home, then a bit after set off to find 'em again. Anyway, they walked it and I says, "Well I went up to Crooked Spire, where I said I'd pick you up, that end." He said, "Ah, we were just sat there resting." I know what they were doing – they'd had too much to drink! That were just one incident.

You couldn't have any lights. You had side lights and you had to cut a hole the size of a penny for light to come out. Then you had to put a mask over your headlamps. It was made of cardboard cut into bars. You had to take glass out and fit 'em in. And it just made bit of light you'd got fall to floor. Ah, all cars were fitted with that, buses and all. Of course, everything kept running as normal, but what spoilt it was when paratroopers came in Hardwick Park. There was a big barracks up there. They used to make bit of a fool of themselves in pubs and that. They reckon that Hardwick ponds were half-full of bikes, they used to pinch bikes and ride 'em – sling 'em into pond. Aye, they were a rum lot they were. When it got to nine o'clock they used to take all buses off the road. It were bad for everybody."

DAIRY FARMING

"The milk squirted in to the empty bucket and as the milk built up
it turned into froth and it made a different noise then.
Ah, they were days to look back on."

Besides the arable work, which was done mainly by Howard, there were the dairy cows to care for. Every morning and evening they had to be milked. Morning milking meant early rising.

"In days when we were hand milking it was a slow job and originally, when I was a little lad, we had to take our milk down to Stretton to catch a train to Sheffield. This train used to be in Stretton station at half-past seven every morning, so me father'd have to be up soon after five o'clock, to get his

milking done and his milk loaded up and taken down to the station. And they'd be big, lumbering 17 gallon churns in those days. Early on, me father was one of the first to have a car and he had the back cut out and made a big door in the back. Somebody did it for him, so that he could load his milk churn up into this old car and get down to Stretton Station quicker than taking it with a horse and cart. Because most folks had to do it that way. And that'd be his first job in the morning, get his milk done and get away."

The big, 17 gallon churns at the Co-operative Dairy, Wood St. Derby, 1934.

The ten gallon churns arriving at the Nestles factory, Ashbourne in the1950s.

Later on there would be more than one churn, but they were smaller.

"We never had above three churns altogether. That was when we were in full production. Mostly it was just two churns that we made. Those were ten gallon churns, but the ones that we used to take to Stretton Station, they were 17 gallon churns, tapered ones, narrow at the top and wide at the bottom. They were big ugly churns to handle. But these ten gallon churns, they were a lot better and they came in to being when we stopped sending it by rail and milk lorries came round then. Dairies had their own lorries, and they came round and collected the milk from our yard end at the side of the lane. So we weren't having to get up so early then. They'd perhaps be collecting it, half-past nine, half-past ten time in the morning, so it was a lot better. At one time though, we bottled our own milk. My father's cousin had a milk round in Tupton, he took our milk.

In the 1947 winter we couldn't get the milk away. In the snow the lorry couldn't pick the milk up. We'd perhaps two, three, four day's milk hanging about … we used to drag it up to the top of the lane, with a horse and sledge. The tractor was no good in that snow so we used the horse for that all the time. We used to put these churns at the top of the lane on the main road side and just hope he was able to get to it. Sometimes they'd stand there two or three days and they took no harm because they were frozen. It actually froze in the churns, it was so cold. Then he'd come eventually and collect all these churns and he'd happen leave four or five more for us to go back again. They were the Dairy's churns, and all that we did was tie a label on to the handle with our name and the number of gallons of milk in the churn and they just took the label off and recorded it at their end. That's how they worked it."

In the earlier years, the cows would be milked by hand. It was a skill taught by father to son.

"My father, he'd milked all his life, so it was just a natural thing that I picked up from him. I did quite a lot of hand milking. We didn't get a milking machine till 1952, I think, so up till then we were hand-milking. My father, my mother and me as well, we all did it. My father used to turn his cap round to the side of his head and shove his head into the cow's side. The front of his cap was all greasy from the beasts."

Some cows were more amenable than others.

"They weren't all easy, no. There were some that we called "easy-milked" and there were some "hard-milked". Some of them, you'd a job to squeeze the milk out, it was so hard to get it out. And cows didn't seem to mind but oh, it did make your hand ache. I was never a fast milker, I don't think I ever did above four in an hour. My mother was a lot faster than me, she could get through six in an hour, but she used to say, in her later years, that the continued squeezing had brought arthritis into her fingers. And my father, I think he might have been a bit quicker than me, but I was the slowest of the lot. But I did manage it. And of course there were quiet cows and there were cows that kicked you over as well. It was not a very safe job sometimes. Very often young cows and first calved heifers, they could be really nasty and, well, they'd kick you over and bucket and milk and everything'd go flying. You were in danger of getting hurt sometimes. It wasn't always a very nice job. They weren't all quiet, contented animals. But we accepted it as it was then, in them days, it was farming as it was."

Sometimes the cows were milked in the field as John Heathcote remembers.

"I were about seven year old. And these fields were away from the farm in Brassington where me grandfather lived at that particular time. And, I remember, I'd got to learn to milk these cows. Well, when it were summertime they used to put so many churns in a horse and float and go to fields with buckets and stools, and the cows were in field and you went and sat down under a cow and you milked 'em. They weren't fastened up, they'd just stand there and we used to milk them in middle of field."

A wry description of the technique and difficulties of hand milking is given by Miss Bassett.

Milking in the fields.

"Before milking machines came in we milked by hand. Yes. I guess there are not many women can do it nowadays in Ashover. How did I do it? Well I got a three-legged stool and sat down and just milked away."

Mrs Hole explains that

"The cows had corn put in their mangers, it kept them occupied whilst being milked."

Miss Bassett continues:

"You put the bucket between your knees and balance yourself on a three-legged stool. That was quite a work of art...it didn't make your hands sore, in fact they got rather nice and soft, I think. But I've never been a person that can do things with gloves on or mittens or anything like that. I like to have my fingers free. And you know, a three-legged stool isn't always the easiest thing to sit on. And in the cow byre, it wasn't all clean or anything like that; the stool could slip away from underneath you. And I've sat down many a time in the cow byre. And the cows just upset the bucket or something like that. But that was long before milking machines. Now

Milking. This young woman feels safer not balanced on a three legged stool.

the milk doesn't see the light of day at all. I wasn't the only
milker of course. There was the farm manager and I think we
employed two men otherwise. And oh, I was rather slow, I
think. If I did two or three at milking time, that was as much
as I could manage, whereas they'd do four or five. I only wish
I could do a bit more now than I do…it's more of an effort to
sit still than to do any work"

The milk then had to be cooled. At Howard's farm there was a
cooler.
"It was made of metal, it was corrugated, and water ran
through the inside and the milk ran down these corrugations.
It'd be about 18 inches wide and perhaps a little bit higher,
longer, upwards, and there'd be a trough in the top of it and a
trough at the bottom and above the cooler there was a big pan
with a tap on it. We poured milk into this big pan and opened
the tap and just regulated it to a steady flow and the milk ran
down these corrugations while the cold water was running
through the inside. And then the churn was underneath with a
sile, to filter the milk. We called it a sile, it was like a big dish
with a filter in the bottom of it that cleaned all the bits out. And
then the milk was cool when it was in the churn. That's all
there was to it at that time."

For Olive, working on the farm at Ault Hucknall, cooling the milk
entailed hard physical work.
"They had a pump on the sink, and they used to cool the milk
themselves, and you'd got to fill this tank that were outside. I
know I once counted how many times you had to go up and
down, up and down with this pump. I remember one time I'd got
a carbuncle under me arm so that were no picnic. No it weren't."

Arthur Hind agrees. Before machinery was introduced he would
daily fill a two hundred gallon tank with water to cool the milk
churns, turning the pump handle endlessly.

Joe Holmes remembers the milk cooler as a modern innovation.
"Ah, Unwin had first little cooler I ever saw. He came to
Milltown Farm in about 1921 I think. Milk run down outside,
onto ridge steel things and water inside running through.

That's how they cooled it."
Before this rather primitive piece of machinery became available
there was a simpler method for cooling the milk. As Joe says, they
"Used to stand churns in trough in summer, that's how they
cooled it in summer. And, if it weren't a deep trough, you had
a smaller churn."

Later on the milk was cooled automatically. The advance to
machine milking was not always welcomed. When the machines
first came in they were installed by a firm called Laval. Fred Hole
recalls.
"The man in charge would have bed and breakfast
accommodation until the farmer was confident enough to
tackle it on his own."

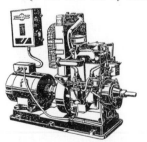
There was one farmer who lived in Lea who brought the milking units for Fred to sort out for him. He was known for his brash language.
"He plonked it all down onto our kitchen floor and said "Sort that bugger out!". He was quite a character. In those days farmers didn't take kindly to changes, but the young farmers of today cope nicely, especially with machinery."

Howard's father was not impressed either. "When we'd machine milking, me father never liked it. He always used to prefer hand milking 'em. It was generally my job to do it. If I was busy on other work, he would use it, but I don't think he liked it. I think he'd the idea that a machine didn't milk 'em clean out. He always used to go round 'em all by hand after, just to make sure he'd got all the milk out. Nobody else bothered with anything like that, but he'd be there under these cows, trying 'em all to see if there was any milk left in them. And of course it made them hang on to the milk then, because they expected him going round and letting last drops out. No, he didn't like to think that machine did it all. Nowadays it's all automatic. I don't know how they cope with it – I mean you get cows with mastitis. I don't know how they sort it out, when it's all machine operated.

When we hand milked, with a bucket between our knees, the milk squirted in to the empty bucket and then as the milk built up it turned into froth and it made a different noise then. Ah, they were days to look back on."

When the milk had been delivered to the station, Howard's father would have more work to do.

"He'd get back home again and then he'd feed all his cows round after that. That'd be the first job. And then, after that, he'd get in for his own breakfast. That'd be the last one to be fed! Of course, in that time it was always bacon and egg for breakfast in the morning. And my mother'd be in the house getting breakfast ready, and I should be packed off to school. (I should walk up to Ashover School at that time, because there'd be no buses or anything. And we used to enjoy walking. Nothing else for us.) And then after me father'd had his breakfast, he'd go out and he'd have some more yard jobs to do, mucking all the sheds out and perhaps feeding them round again. First of all, they'd just have a feed of hay before he went in for his breakfast. And then he'd go out after his breakfast.

We had lots of small sheds with perhaps three, four, five animals in each shed and he always turned his cattle out every day, for exercise. We never kept them tied up all day. They all went out, apart from little calves. The stirks, as we called them, (the middle ones), and the milk cows were all turned out every day for a bit of exercise, even in winter. They were out of the way, and, till we had water bowls in the shed, they'd got to go out to drink, to the trough outside. All the milk cows'd go out together. They'd go to the field, to the trough and drink and have a bit of a walk round and a scratch and rub, while he or I mucked them out and fed them round. Then they came in again and they settled down for the rest of the day then. And then he'd move to another little shed and there'd be three or four turned out and they'd get the same treatment again. It was far better to turn 'em out, to get an empty shed to work in because they'd be standing on the muck in with the straw. You couldn't get in very well, when they were inside. All the sheds had to be mucked out with a shovel and barrow. It was a time-consuming job, that was. Wheel this muck out into the yard and shoot it up and pile it up in the yard, and all the fodder carried in, in armfuls or forkfuls.

It took all day for one man to do that. He hadn't time to do anything else. And so, while he was doing all the yard work, I was doing the land work for him. And then they'd be fed with corn and most likely mangolds or turnips and them some more hay in their rack and each shed had to be treated like that. And of course by time he'd gone all round every animal, it'd be dinner time."

The food had to be prepared and taken to the animals.
"We'd got a pulper. I've spent some hours winding the handle, pulping mangolds, till I got fed up with it and we bought an engine and coupled the engine to it. You could only put perhaps two turnips in at once, or you wouldn't be able to turn the handle. But it wasn't long in pulping a good big heap underneath it. It scooped the turnips – so you got bits, like cheese gratings, only a bigger scale, that fell out underneath.

Then there was the cake breaker – you used to buy slabs of cake. They'd be about two feet wide and four feet long and about one and a half feet thick. You fed the slab of cake into a slot on the top of the cake breaker and turned the handle and it'd crush the slab and it'd slide down a chute into a tub and all the fine stuff went through a riddle and dropped under-neath into a little box. And we should feed the fine stuff to calves and the bigger lumps – they'd be roughly the size of your thumb – to the cows. We bought the compressed cake at White's in Clay Cross. They were cattle feed folks, right at the corner of Broadley's, straight opposite the Salvation Army. They were grocers, but they'd everything in the feed line for the farmers. They used to deliver and I think we'd another firm as well. We'd perhaps two or three people delivered cattle feed to us. They used to bring these big slabs of cotton cake that they called it.

And there was hay to be cut, with the old cutting knife. It was for cutting trusses of hay out. I've spent some hours working that up and down when we used to get hay loose. Because that was the only way of getting it out of the stack. You cut square blocks out, I should say two foot six square, something like that. It'd be anywhere between a foot and 18 inches deep. You cut the depth of the blade, but if you got the full depth, you'd a big heap of hay on your back. So you regulated it to how much you could carry. But I always used to carry it with a fork. Stick a fork into the truss of hay and just pull it over on to me back and carry it that way. But I've known lots of old farmers, they'd lift the edge of the block of hay up and get their head under it and work their head underneath 'till they'd got it onto the back of their shoulders. And then I think they got a rope over the top to hold it on and they carried it that way. But it'd be a bit of an uncomfortable job I think. It was a lot easier to stick a fork in and just pull it over on to your back.

We would have to cut quite a lot of hay. Our stacks, they'd be perhaps 14 or 16 feet high, under the hay barn. You'd start at the top and you'd perhaps come half way down for a day's fodder. Our main cow-shed held 12 cows and there was a chamber above it. I should perhaps carry eight or ten squares of this hay into the chamber itself to feed the milk cows. And then there'd be all the other little buildings with other stock in and I should have to carry a truss round to them as well and drop it in a dry corner somewhere, to feed them. And that'd be practically every day. Sometimes, it'd last, perhaps two days. But we should be cutting hay every day for some of 'em. And it was quite a big job, that."

Other jobs would have to be fitted into a day.

"Then me father'd have his dinner and after that he'd have chance to go into a field and perhaps do some field work, either muck carting or ploughing or something like that, dependent on the season. He'd come in for his tea at night and then it'd be milking again. When it went dark, we'd always something else to do in yard, particularly in winter when all cows were in. I should happen go ploughing till it went dark and come home and we should have our tea and start milking, particularly when it was hand milking."

For these mixed farms the work with the animals and caring for them was a ceaseless round, as Miss Bassett explains.

"You fed the cows in the morning. And in the winter time, of course you couldn't turn them out into the fields so they had to have a second go in the middle of the day. And then you gave them another good feed at night time. It was always rather like the human household. When you've had your breakfast, you're preparing lunch ready. You eat that and you get your next meal ready. It's everlasting. But in a farmer's life you see, it would be interspersed with a milking session. And you had to milk by hand. That was a great job. Hard work too. You couldn't neglect it and one day say, "Oh I won't bother with that today, I'll do that tomorrow." You had to do it, or else there would be an episode of some sort. Either the poor old animal would collapse or want attention."

Sycamore Farm was fairly typical:

"We hadn't a big herd," says Millie Ablett.

A considerable amount of work was involved nevertheless.

"In those days, there were only small individual sheds, not like the cowsheds they've got today. That did come later, but at that time, we'd a cowshed at the bottom of the yard held eight and then another at the top. That had four in. And they had chambers over the top and you threw the hay down to feed them. And then there was another little shed further down the yard and that held five. So we'd always got them full. I got married when I was 23 and after I was married, they did have a big cowshed put up, because by then we'd got electricity."

Evening milking in the winter was a cosy job for the Davisons.
"It was a real nice job in winter, milking cows. You were in the
warm cowshed and the cow's tits were warm, milk was warm.
You were ever so warm. They were tied up in these stand-ins
in the cow-shed on a concrete floor, but there was a bit of
bedding under 'em, dry and warm. There was nothing nicer
than going into that cow shed in the middle of winter, when it
was freezing outside. It was ever so warm. And they were
comfortable – with feed in their mangers. These milking
parlours, they're miserable cold places. And they've got to be
so clean everywhere now. They've got to be washed out and
scrubbed every day. And everywhere's wet and cold. Oh,
they're not nice places at all. No, it's a different environment
altogether for cattle and men as well to work in. We milked by
paraffin lamps. You just carried them round with you, just
hung 'em up in the cow shed on a convenient nail while you
milked. We knew nothing else, we were used to groping about
in darkness – the gas didn't come till 1937. We thought it was
marvellous when they brought the gas. We had it in the house
and in the main cow shed as well. The gas lamp in the cow
shed was hung over one of the windows and it shone straight
across the yard into the dairy. It was very convenient."

In fact, working with the animals was so enjoyable that Howard's
father would be pottering about till bed-time.
"Perhaps sometimes, till half-past ten, eleven o'clock at night,
and me mother'd wonder where he'd got to and she'd happen
say to me, "Go out and see where your father is, what's
happened to him." He'd be poking about, bedding some cows
down or giving them a bit of something, or looking round 'em
and making sure they were all right. He lived for his cattle.
That was his sole enjoyment. I think they'd all got names, by
time they were milk cows. None of the young ones had. Oh, he
did enjoy his cattle. And a final feed, round of his cattle and
into bed. That'd be his day's work, in winter."

Milking in the hours of darkness was lit by candle light before
electricity came to the farms. Fred Hole remembers that in winter
time candles would be put in a recess of the wall so that he could
see to hand milk. Later the task would be done with the aid of a

paraffin lamp hung on a convenient nail in the cowshed.

Although candle light might seem romantic, Miss Lennox is clear that it was sometimes far from comfortable.

"In '47, it was so cold, that the pipes with the milk coming to the tank froze up beside me while I was writing in the dairy. I was so bitterly cold, I used to stuff my Wellington boots with hay. And we were working with candles – there was no electricity. There were always two or three candles for me to write by, stuck in the cowshed window."

Work would be easier in the summertime, resumes Howard:

"In summer cows'd be turned out to grass, so he'd not have all this feeding and mucking out to do. Cows get used to a certain field and they'd not need much driving. Well, we used to drive our milk cows from our place to Brown Lane. Every day – take 'em down in the morning and fetch them back at night. They'd just amble down. You had to prod 'em sometimes if they stopped, they seemed to know their way. We shouldn't have anyone to turn 'em at Brown Lane end. They'd know which field it was they'd to go into. And the same coming back, they'd just walk home. There were no motors to bother 'em in them days. We used to take 'em down to them fields against Greyhound as well. When we'd milked we should turn 'em out and they'd go up that field at the back of our house, out on to main road and down to the fields at Greyhound to graze."

The milking might be left to Howard's mother.

"I remember in summer, during the war, when we were very busy and me and me father were happen contracting as well, corn cutting, she'd milk all our cows herself. She'd get them in after she'd had a bit of tea. The cows (there were only about nine) would come up on their own. They'd be waiting to come in to be milked and all she'd need to do would be open field gate and let 'em in and tie them up. They'd go in to their stalls and they'd all be tied up so they couldn't come out again 'till she let 'em out. They'd have a chain round their neck. She'd put a bit of corn in each manger, to tempt 'em to come in while she got them tied up and she'd just milk 'em all and turn 'em all out again and they'd just wander off down in the fields and settle down then, for the night. And she'd just have the tackle and the milking things, to wash up. Before we had a milking machine, it would only be a bucket that she'd have to wash, and the milk cooler. Of course, later on, when we had a milking machine, she'd use that instead. She'd be able to milk a lot quicker with that on her own. She got as she could manage the milking machine as well. Because she'd only got to switch on the electricity and then just carry the units in and milk that way."

One summer time job was putting the young beasts out to summer pasturage.

"Aye, – and this particular morning, me mother and me used to set off with these cattle, (we should take seven or eight) and we should drive 'em. Usually we went up Overton with them, because it was a quiet road, and out on to top of Slack and right along that road towards Beeley. And then me father, he'd do rest of his jobs, feeding the milk cows round and mucking out and things like that and then he'd follow in his car and he'd catch us up somewhere towards Beeley Moor. And very often then, we should start joining up with other lots going. And take 'em right down into bottom of Chatsworth and then up through the park. And then we should go through a gate, through that wood on the left-hand side into what they called Calton Lees. And there, they'd these branding sheds and we should all gather up our own cattle and these chaps'd be branding them. They'd hot irons with a certain number on for each farmer's cattle. And, in them days, all cattle had horns and so they were branded on their horns with a number. That's how we were able to identify them, when we fetched 'em out at autumn, and we should drive 'em back home same as we took 'em. And we seemed to have no trouble in them days. There was no traffic at all to contend with. And another thing, most folks shut their gates and we'd not so much trouble with cattle straying. Nowadays, it'd be impossible, because they'd be in everybody's garden all the way there. We couldn't manage it. But at that time, it was a different life altogether. I remember one summer, they had a bad thunderstorm in Chatsworth and lightening struck one of our beasts and killed it. And we had to go up and identify it and – I don't know what happened. It'd be disposed of. There were no trouble getting rid of them in them days. Local knacker man'd fetch it and cut it up for dog meat. There were no forms to fill in or anything at that time, nobody to bother you. If we'd thought we could have brought it home and eaten it! Nobody'd have cared. Eh, it was a different life altogether."

When John Heathcote was working for his grand-father at Brassington the cows they had
"at that time were called shorthorns. Nowadays, if you see a herd of beasts they'll all be black and white or all red or what-ever. They were a pretty mixed lot but they were classed as shorthorns."

Other farms had pedigree herds. At the Bassetts' farm the cows were known as the Ashover Blue Herd. They were Blue Albions and were taken to shows. A Milltown resident, Geoff Hammond, whose sister worked as a maid for the Bassetts describes the preparations this involved.
"The cows which were to be shown had to have strong bands round their heads to train their horns. These bands were of leather, one and a half inches wide and a quarter of an inch thick."

Miss Bassett says the bands were used to keep their horns growing to the front. If necessary the horns had to be filed to shape. They were pedigree animals so they'd got a longer history with their names.

Chatsworth Park

and

Calton Pastures Agistment

1936.

Mr. *B. Davidson* .... No. *39* ......

Number	HORSES—		£	s.	d.	Amount due
....	Two Years old..............................@		3	0	0	
....	One Year old ....@		2	10	0	
	CATTLE—					
....	Cow or Stirk over 2½ Year old @		2	5	0	
....	Stirk over 1½ Years old.......@		1	15	0	
6	Calves under 1½ Years old.......@		1	7	6	8 5
		Total amount due		8	5	

Taking-out day, Wednesday, Oct. 7th.
This Card must be brought, and the charge for Agistment paid at the time of taking out the Cattle.

Cheques to be made payable to F. G. C. Hartopp.

For further particulars apply to :—
THE AGENT, ESTATE OFFICE, CHATSWORTH, BAKEWELL ; *or* MR. J. McLAUCHLAN, EDENSOR, BAKEWELL.

Bradbourne Bella, a Hilltop farm Blue Albion.
She won first prizes at Bakewell and Ashover shows in 1927.

On Sycamore Farm

"The majority of the cows were Ayrshires. There were one or two that had names. Sam had a special cow named Daisy and some of them had got names that they shouldn't perhaps have had at times, if they'd decided to kick. The majority were pretty placid, though you did get the odd one that decided it didn't like being milked. When they had just calved, they'd be tender, then they'd get a bit frisky. And I remember once, my sister who worked at Ambergate, came home (she was in service). She wanted to be big stuff and let the cows out and I'd changed into a summer dress – I always wore knee breeches to work on the farm – and I walked up between these cows. I was going to tell my brother that Isobel would let them out. And a cow took fright because I'd got a dress on. It broke the boskin, caught me on the leg – could easily have broken my leg and took off down the yard with the chain round its neck. Poor Isabel thought it was her fault but I suppose it was partly my fault, because the cows weren't used to seeing me in a light-coloured dress. Of course, when you didn't have so many, they were individual cows, whereas today they are just a number."

April 7th 1977.

Ayrshire Heifer.

The Hellaby cows were named. Among them were Emma, Pansie, Grace, Olive, Eve, Dolly, Gertie, Nellie, Silvia, Susan, Erica, Honey and Trixie.

In his diary Ted Hellaby gives a little history of Olive's difficult time.

11 May 1931 Olive picked her calf (cow calf). Buried calf in Browsey field. (picked means miscarried.)

5 June Olive taken bad with milk fever.

6 June. Olive rather better.

New arrivals were noted:

10 May 1931. Lottie calved cow calf. (Nancy.)

Sundays seem to have been the preferred day, for on 9 August "Diania" calved cow calf Jean. And on Harvest Festival Sunday, Topsy calved. June, (as Olive had), picked her calf on September

first. Perhaps Freda was a special favourite. She calved on 14 May
and had her picture drawn.

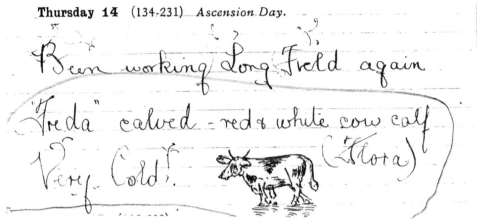

Thursday 14 (134-231) *Ascension Day.*

Been working Long Field again

"Freda" calved - red & white cow calf
Very Cold.   (Flora)

Having favourites could be traumatic as John Heathcote recalls.
"We used to hand milk about 40 something cows at that
particular time and when you got a lot like that, you treat 'em
all alike, treat em all properly – or you should. They didn't
have names, no. There were only two as had. Two cows me
grandfather had, up at Gladwin Mark, and they were what
you call roan 'uns, red and white, mixed. Two very old cows.
These were two as he'd reared from calves and one were 16
and one were a bit more than that. And these vets came round
and they were testing for cattle with TB. They'd inject them
and come again after so long, measure everything up, and if
the cows had reacted to the injections they were destroyed.
Me grandfather nearly went mad because these two were
very old and very bony and they both reacted to the injections
and they had to go. He nearly went mad. They had been with
him for years...."

Howard describes de-horning – a job that was becoming less
necessary.
"Well, originally, when cows had big horns, they used to saw
'em off, or use huge clippers, like big bolt cutters and chop 'em
off. They'd long handles on them because it takes no end of
pressure to chop the horn off. But sawing them off, that was
worse than ever, because it was a slower job. There was no
end of blood flying about then. Of course it dried on and

October 5ᵀᴴ
1975.

congealed and it'd be a week or two before it finally got rubbed off. And sometimes, I think they used to cauterize them with a hot iron to stop 'em bleeding. But it was a rotten, messy job. And of course, as it got more popular, this de-horning, they used to do them as little calves, de-bud 'em as they called it – they'd inject an anaesthetic into the horn bud first and get a specially shaped hot iron and just scoop this horn bud out. And calf never bothered about it at all.

When they had horns it encouraged them fight each other.
"If they were going to be aggressive, they'd face up to one another. One cow'd boss everybody else about and other cows'd fancy their chances and they'd have a right fight. When they fought, very often they'd rip the skin and it'd bleed. They'd do a bit of damage to one another. Sometimes, they'd get their horn into the other one's ribs and make, not deep cuts but they fetched the hair off and a bit of skin as well. Eventually one'd happen get a horn broken off in the process and that'd quieten them off, they'd slink away then. But there was always a boss cow amongst them, when they'd got horns, and at feeding time, in loose troughs or anything of that sort, they'd get the best of everything. They'd shove everybody else out with these wicked horns. And of course, now that cows have no horns at all, they stand quite happily together, bunched together and they're more peaceful alto-gether. There's no aggressiveness at all. They might just butt

one or two with their head, but there's no damage done at all. It was a good job when they de-horned cattle."

Even more alarming than the horned cattle, Eva Butler remembers a necessary if intimidating companion for the cows: "There was a bull at Sycamore farm at one time. And I can remember, Bill said they found it on the yard. It could get its horn under the latch and let itself out. And I thought, "My word! I hope I don't meet it on the road.""

Mavis Hind had a much closer encounter with a bull. It was a hired bull. The men did not bring it until dusk. The Hinds had carefully checked all the field gates on the roadside. The cows however, were not too happy with the newcomer, and, to escape from them, he had pushed and pulled at the gate of the field so hard that it bent. The

Oct 16TH 1977.

gatepost at one side came out of the ground, the gate opened and out came the bull. He came down the yard to the farmhouse. Mr and Mrs Hind, sitting in the parlour thought they heard a tapping at the kitchen door. Mrs Hind went to the door, opened it, shut it quickly and called "You'd better come and see – and be prepared for a shock." When they opened the door the bull was quite placid. They led him to an empty shed where he settled happily, away from his tormentors.

Occasionally a cow might need doctoring.

"There was a chap came round from a firm who sold various bottles of drink and stuff that we horned down them," says Howard. "The favourite thing was one called "All in One". I don't know what was in it, but it was very potent stuff. You could smell it and it was ever such strong stuff. And there was one or two other bottles of stuff that me father use to have in stock. There was White Oils, that was perhaps an embrocation for horses. Then there was Stockholm Tar. It was sticky, black, tarry stuff. After we'd milked in a morning in summer, we had a tin of Stockholm Tar and a little wooden stick to dip in, to dab it on the end of each tit, if it had a cut or a graze on it, to stop flies. (They caused mastitis.) At night of course we didn't bother. It might have had some healing properties as well. We had linseed oil too, it was a laxative. If a cow was "bun-up" we'd horn it down 'em.

Sometimes a cow 'd break its horn off and in those days, the shorthorns, some of them, had quite big horns

on. They'd be perhaps a foot long and a curved horn as well.
And we should save this horn and it'd be hollowed out.
There'd be nothing inside it. And we'd use that to give them
these drinks. We'd fill the horn with this stuff and we horned
it down 'em. That's where the name comes from. And I
remember me father wrapping his arm round a cow's head
and hoisting it up in the air and stuffing this horn into the
cow's mouth and hoping it swallowed it. A bit of a messy job.
I remember very often he used to tie an old bag down the
front of him because more often than not the cow spewed it
back on to him and he got it all down the front of him, so he
usually had an old bag tied down to protect him. I can
remember that quite vividly but I never did the job at all. No.
If these "All in Ones" didn't cure 'em, it was the vet's job."

Howard's father would also treat his cattle when they had been
attacked by warble flies, applying dressing and squeezing the
grubs from their hide.

"He'd squeeze and gradually work this thing out – it'd be as
big as my thumb. They spoilt the hide, for leather. These flies,
the cows could hear them coming, they made a horrible
buzzing noise. It used to drive the cattle crazy. They'd go
tearing round the pasture fields with these flies coming after
them. They knew what to expect from these horrible buzzing
flies. They'd settle on their back and lay their eggs and it
must have been painful even then."

A cow which was mildly unwell could be treated with a tonic. As
Bert Hopkinson says:

"There were several firms selling cattle medicine, some of
which was quite good as a pick-me-up. One firm was Leonard
Smith & Co. Blackheath, Birmingham. Their local represen-
tative was Jack Young. He would breeze in during morning
milking, get out his notebook and sell us six bottles of All-in-
One, a universal cure. (Some of his customers took it themselves!) After drenching a cow with it the smell hung round
the shed for days. He always had a tent at local farm shows,
where his customers could get a cup of tea and a sit down. He
stood near the entrance and out came his notebook as each
customer left giving him an order for six bottles of All-in-One

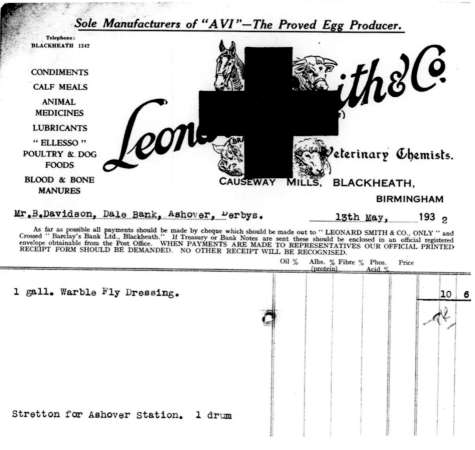

Sole Manufacturers of "AVI"—The Proved Egg Producer.

Telephone:
BLACKHEATH 1242

CONDIMENTS

CALF MEALS

ANIMAL
MEDICINES

LUBRICANTS

" ELLESSO "
POULTRY & DOG
FOODS

BLOOD & BONE
MANURES

Leon...ith&Co.

Veterinary Chemists.

CAUSEWAY MILLS, BLACKHEATH,

BIRMINGHAM

Mr.B.Davidson, Dale Bank, Ashover, Derbys.　　13th May, 193 2

As far as possible all payments should be made by cheque which should be made out to " LEONARD SMITH & CO., ONLY " and Crossed " Barclay's Bank Ltd., Blackheath." If Treasury or Bank Notes are sent these should be enclosed in an official registered envelope obtainable from the Post Office.　WHEN PAYMENTS ARE MADE TO REPRESENTATIVES OUR OFFICIAL PRINTED RECEIPT FORM SHOULD BE DEMANDED.　NO OTHER RECEIPT WILL BE RECOGNISED.

	Oil %	Albs. % (protein)	Fibre %	Phos. Acid %	Price
1 gall. Warble Fly Dressing.					10 6
Stretton for Ashover Station. 1 drum					

to add to his mounting stocks at home. Jack was a great character."

Nowadays the drugs are different and more powerful, but they can
have adverse effects on the milk. Formerly milk might be tainted,
but if the milk was being collected for a dairy, it did not seem to
matter, thinks Howard!
"In the old days you could tell, from the taste of the milk,
when they'd been in that wild garlic. Oh, that was terrible
stuff, that was. You could smell the cows when they came in,
their breath smelt and the milk – it wasn't fit to drink you
know. It was terrible, it tainted it ever so badly. And there
were other things, not so bad – when they'd been eating kale,
you could taste it then. It was a different flavour when they'd
had kale to eat.
But the milk went. It seemed to go in those days. I don't know

what happened at the other end, at the dairies. I suppose they happen poured it into everybody else's and it got diluted till it passed as fit to drink. It wouldn't now. You can try to keep the cows off the garlic till it's died off, or spray it to try to kill it a bit, but you can't eradicate it. It's such a shiny leaf on it. It doesn't absorb chemicals. It's an awful job to kill it off. And the smell is so powerful."

Grazing Kale.
Oct. 5th 1986

But, on the whole, Howard considers that the old methods

"Didn't do any harm. The milk was clean. Good quality. It was filtered and cooled and it was perfectly good. No, nowadays, if the inspector sees a cobweb in the milking parlour, it's a crime. And you mustn't have a fly in summer in the parlour. And you're not allowed to have any swallows nesting any-where near where they're milking cows. While we were milking the places were full of swallows. Yes, we'd swallows' nests everywhere. They did no harm. They've got so hygienic now that people have no resistance. A lot of people, they don't know what fresh milk is. It's all heat treated and sterilized and pasteurised and homogenised. Everything's taken out of it. It's nothing better than glorified whitewash."

Miss Lennox remembers with approval those more relaxed days. "They were always considerate with the wild life. One farm I went to, at Buckland Hollow, was having a cowshed renovated, to have more milkers. It was summer time, and they were managing outside. They apologized – "well, next time well have a roof over for you". And so, I went next time and it wasn't finished, nowhere like finished. I asked "What happened, did the builders go on holiday?" They said, "the swallows hadn't gone. We couldn't have it done and turn the swallows out. It would be bad luck".

Quality and cleanliness were all important. Milk was food for a child who was not strong. Dorothy Ward remembers:

"A friend of the family had a rather delicate daughter. When they visited, the little girl would come into the cowshed with her mug. "I've come for my milk" and she would drink it straight from the cow. We always washed the cows' udders. They were very clean."

Lucy Moore used to fetch the milk from Goodalls on Ashover Hay.

"They always used to wear mob caps and aprons in the dairy. It always struck me, as a child, as being very clean."

Howard, whose interest lay in the arable side of the work of the farm, was never quite so interested in the animals.

"After me father died, if cows were ill it was the vet every time. Me father, he was a real stock man. He enjoyed his cattle, rather than arable work and ... well, he lived for them, night and day. He didn't want to go out anywhere, or anything. We never thought of holidays. No. No. If, me father might manage a day, we'd go to Skegness in the car, and that was a big day out for us. We'd got to get up extra early in the morning to get milked and cleared up and leave the farm man to do the essential jobs, while we had a day at Skegness. It was a bit of a rush job."

PIGS

"They weren't the little pigs that you see nowadays.
The biggest we had was forty two stone. It was a monster."

Whether the farm was a dairy or arable one, pigs were an important source of income. And others besides farmers, if they had the room and the means, kept a pig.

After Lily Barker's family moved to a cottage at Northedge her father

"Built a makeshift pig sty (no planning regulations then) and I remember the arrival of our first piglet. My father had walked with it in a sack-bag on his back from Alton which I

A cottager's pig.

thought was very cruel but which didn't lessen my excitement at the arrival of this lovely piglet to add to the few hens we had."

Roma Unwin's pig arrived in an even more novel way. She and her sister won it at a big garden party at Marsh Green.

"It was about three foot long, in a wooden box and it was called Sago, and Joe Hole gave it, from up Slack. Anyway, we won this pig, it was a lovely little pig. We walked from Marsh Green, carrying it. It was in a wooden box with handles on. Peggy and I brought this pig right down Church Street. And I was going part-time to Walton Back Lane where my husband-to-be lived. They'd stables because he was a butcher. He got another one to go with it. I used to feed these every morning, I would never have had any bacon or anything from them. Anyway one Wednesday (they'd grown into great big pigs) they'd sent them .... oh I was cross. They were lovely."

During World War II a pig made a big difference to your standard of living. Like many others at the time, the Eatons had a "family pig."

"We reared a little pig and some months after had it killed, so we were all right then." Ellen Eaton's daughter in law, Betty Dimbleby recalls

"Well you were allowed actually to buy two, but you could only keep one yourself. One had to go to the bacon factory or somewhere. And then I think you got some sort of allowance of meat or something."

Mrs Eaton remembers that while they were rearing the pig it became a family pet.

"It used to jump up on the door and wait. And I'd take a hose pipe and it drank out of the hose pipe. We got very fond of that. But we knew he had to go though, so that was it."

Killing the pig was a dramatic event. Olive's parents kept several pigs. Their pig killer was Johnny Newbold. Once, when he came to decide which of the pigs to kill, he opened only the bottom half of the stable-type door. One of the pigs bolted and went straight between his bandy legs. It took him with it, round the croft. He was sitting on it backwards, holding on by its tail. The tighter he gripped, the faster it went. His bandy legs just fitted round the pig as if made to measure!

Once you were master of the situation, though, there were various ways of killing the pig, some more accept-able than others. Joe remembers:

The family pig.

> "A bloke named Davenport were rummest fellow I ever saw pig killing. Used to drive 'em to nearest tree and then hang them up wi' back legs. Then cut their throats. He used to fasten his pulley in tree, then fetch pig, where he wanted. And then get its back legs and hang it up and pull it up and while it were hanging up, he used to kill it. He hadn't got a pig form. He used to scrape 'em while they were hanging up. Then cut 'em up while they were there. Cut 'em up and take hams and things off 'em. He did it for a bit of a side line."

Joe concedes that this might not have been the ideal method.
> "Oh well, they don't allow it now. All have to go to the abattoir now."

His own pigs were killed in a different way.
> "I bought three off a mate o' mine at Hepthorne Lane. I had some down where father-in-law lived. Me and father in law always had pigs there. Have three, kill one and sell two. I've held some pigs while they've been stuck. There's no pig-killing now. I mean used to kill your own pigs then."

A pig killing at Tansley.

It was not an easy job for various reasons. Perhaps the pigs sensed what was about to happen.

"But – that was it. Quicker you'd got on, the quicker you'd done with it. Jack Bown, he used to kill 'em. Lived up Butterley. He used to go round killing pigs. All these little smallholders had a pig or two, everybody killed a pig a year. I've held pigs while he's killed 'em. Ah, I've held 'em, not killed 'em but held 'em, by their front legs. Ah, they used to squeal a bit. You have to hold 'em on pig form – proper wooden benches they used to kill 'em on. (Pig forms, they called 'em.) I've held legs."

John Hodgson points out that the process was not so barbaric as it may seem.

"They talk about cruelty when the pig was slaughtered. When it's slaughtered, it's brought up garden path to kitchen door, because copper's boiling ready for it. Well, all the stress it gets, when it gets up there they trip it up, and first reaction is, "I've got to get on my feet." – He's more interested in getting on his feet, than knowing he's going to have his throat cut, and when throat's cut that's the end of it. Where's the stress factor? Whereas now, he goes into metal trailer and is taken to market, they're frightened to death to go in the truck and stand in the market among strange animals and then they're taken to slaughter house, it's sweated flesh."

Not all pigs were killed by design. At one time Miss Lennox "kept a boar on for one for one of the farmers, he had some of the Landrace when they first came in. Then they decided they wanted it castrated. So I asked the vet to come and do it. He sent a newly qualified young man and got Dick Bown to come and hold it – it was already half grown. He had to give it chloroform over its nose. Which he did, but he put too much and he killed it! Oh, what a commotion! Dick Bown said "Quick, quick, run to the kitchen for a knife. We'll have to cut its throat quickly." The vet killed the pig – but it wasn't wasted, we cut its throat and hung it up quickly. The young vet said to me "Will you telephone the boss, to tell him?" He was too frightened."

The process was more organised at Dale Bank farm.
"Of course during the war time we had pigs. We should have a permit to kill perhaps two pigs a year, something like that. We had a pig form. There was a leg at each corner, like a table, but the top was at least two inches thick, really solid. You stood the pig at the side of it and you reached over it and grabbed a leg a-piece and pulled it on to its back. As quick as that. Before the pig had time to do anything else. You just pulled it, one pair of legs up in the air and dragged him on to

November 15th . To one new plank pig-form
all ash top with oak legs
and 2 long bolts through top . 16.0

To one Cambrel . 2.6

Total = £ 1 .13. 0

the form. That was it.

Then, the pig killer, he'd shoot them, stun them first, and then slit the throat to bleed them. We should collect the blood of course, for black pudding. My mother made no end of black pudding. I can taste that now. It <u>was</u> good. And then, we'd a big copper boiling in the yard, that we used to boil clothes in, for washing, and that was all fired with coal. My mother had got that stoked up and the big copper full of boiling water. Then it was my job carrying buckets of boiling water and pouring it over this pig and they were scraping the hairs off it, cleaning it. And then, it had to be hauled up and cut up into hams, sides and head and all the bits and bobs connected to it. Another job of mine was rubbing salt into the hams, it was a time-consuming job that. My mother used to buy a block of salt – in those days you bought – it'd be about nine inches square and two feet long – a solid block of salt.

They weren't the little pigs you see nowadays.

The Bassetts' farm account book:

March 1923: paid 1s.6d for salt and salt-petre for pig curing.

We should crush the salt up and then we should lay the hams and the flicks, that is the sides, one by one on the salting stones in the pantry. Then it would be my job to rub all this salt into this meat. And my hands, they'd be red-raw. We had to pay particular attention to where the bone joint was in the ham and rub this salt-petre into it as well, to preserve it there. And then it was left to soak in and when it had dried, they were all hung up on the walls and muslin put round them, to stop flies getting into it. The flicks, the big flicks, they'd be about four feet long, because the pigs were big. They weren't the little pigs that you see nowadays. The biggest we had was 42 stone. It was a monster. We had some fat out of that, and bacon. Ah.

Meanwhile it was my mother's job to start cooking – pork pies, and souse, as we called it. And then we fed off that salted meat for the rest of the year. Kept cutting lumps off. It was different flavoured altogether from the bacon, pork we get nowadays.

But I've still got the legacy of salting pigs in that house. The salt stays in the walls permanently, it's there as a fluffy white coating. You'll <u>never</u> get it out. Even in the room on the other side of the pantry the wallpaper would not stay on without a false front of timber and plaster board being fitted."

Pig killing in wartime could be quite a cloak and dagger event.

"I shall never forget once we'd one permit and we'd six pigs hanging up, we'd killed six pigs. All done at night in the dark. Jack Bown, he was the main pig – killer around here.

The Bassetts' farm account book:

February 1924: paid J. Bown 6d for killing pig.

He was a real old character, and he did all our pigs. And one time, we were busy killing this pig in this shed in the yard, and old Jack Hayes from Dicklant, he come down the yard and looks in. He says, "What would tha do if I were inspector?" And Jack Bown comes up to him, he says "I'd slit his throat". And he'd got knife in his hand. And poor old Jack Hayes, he nearly fainted. He thought he were going to kill him. I'll never forget that. But we killed all those pigs and it was all sold on black market, you know, it all went to locals and folks came at night and we got rid of all these pigs. Ah."

ON SHOW

"Oh, it was a show for everybody. It was a very busy day"

To one child Ashover Show was "as important as Christmas time". It began, modestly, in 1925. It styled itself "The 1ˢᵗ Annual Exhibition of the Ashover Agricultural and Horticultural Society". Even by 1931 the exhibiting members had to "reside in the Parish of Ashover or within a 3 mile radius of Ashover Parish Church, except when otherwise stated in the schedule." Later people from further away were included and open classes were added.

TIME TABLE.

Horticultural Judging, 11 a.m. till finished.

Farm Produce, Bread & Tea Cakes Judging, 11 a.m. till finished.

Tent open at 1 p.m. approximately.

Cattle & Sheep Judging, 11-30 a.m. till finished.

Horse Judging, 12 noon till finished.

Turnouts Judging, 2 p.m. till finished.

Parade of Prize Winning Cattle & Horses in the Big Ring, at 3 p.m.

Entries for Racing to be in the Collecting Ring at 3 p.m.

An enormous amount of preparation went on beforehand. One farmer's wife, having washed the show cows with buckets of water, a scrubbing brush and a bar of soap was thankful when, at the end of the evening before the show "there was only the big black bull to wash". Among other things she had boiled the ropes the animals would be held with and whitened them with Blanco.

At last came "1pm on Wednesday September 16ᵗʰ" the time for the first show to open. There were 11 classes and events and the show followed a Timetable.

*Weighing the milk was a solemn business
which demanded a great deal of concentration.*

Cattle had first place. There was a salutary reminder that "Bulls must be rung". An additional prize for the Best cow in Milk was a milk bucket given by Mr W. Francis of Littlemoor. For the cow giving the most weight of milk the prize was given by Mr J Bassett. "Such cows must be milked out clean the night before the Show at 8 o'clock in the presence of a Steward and before 1pm on Show day."

Pigs and sheep were represented as well as mares and plough horses. There was a class too for "Best Farmer's Light Turnout, either spring cart or float" and one for "Best Heavy Turnout". (In 1927 Mr W. Yeomans promised "a pair of steel hames, value 11s.6d for the latter. Farmers could enter Swede or Common Turnips, Kale or White Oats". A money prize might be offered by a company.

Or the prize might be in kind. In 1931 Leonard Smith (Veterinary Chemists of Blackheath) promised "A tin of Blood Salt, value 12s.6d." to the best foal in the show.

Wives might enter their Dairy Produce. There were classes for "Best dishes of White, brown or tinted eggs", "Best 1lb. of butter, slightly salted, not printed." And the "Best couple of

35   Messrs. Dickson & Robinson, Ltd., The King's Seedsmen,
      Cathedral Street, Manchester, offer for the best six
      SWEDES of their "Mancunian" or "Eclipse" with
      roots off, drawn from a crop of not less than one rood.
          1st prize, 5s.; 2nd, 3s. 6d.; 3rd, 2s. 6d.
    Seed to be purchased direct and ordered through their Agent, Mr. J.
  Tipper, Woodside, Stretton, Alfreton.   A Catalogue free with pleasure.

Extract from 1933 catalogue.

ducklings, trussed, ready for table". In 1931 these were "not
drawn, head and feet left on." Or they might show bread or
teacakes or in the Flower Classes enter "six violas, blooms
dissimilar" or a "Bouquet of garden flowers."

The organisers' aspirations for the children were high.

The boys were judged on "Best School Plots". The girls'
school work was also entered as Hilda Hopkinson remembers.

"We did sewing and we entered our work into the Children's
Class at Ashover Show."

Peaceful moments for the Heavy Turnout.

*The tranquil surroundings and the space and calm of the main ring allayed
tensions as the children's pony classes are judged.*

There was a children's class for the "Best Plain-stitched
Garment" and one for "Best Hand – knitted Garment."

No-one was left out. The "Cleanest and Best-Kept Shepherd
Dog" could win a prize. (5s. in 1925.) There was also a class
for the "Best Dog or Bitch any variety". Sports, including an
"Obstacle Bicycle Race for either sex" a "Pony Race" and
"Musical Chairs on horseback" added excitement to the day.

Perhaps the saddest event was the Block Test. The animal, viewed
and literally, weighed up by a succession of people, would be
slaughtered the following week.

At night-time, after the Show, there was horse-racing. Mrs Hole
remembers her Dad would sit her on the wall to watch. "It was
chiefly trotting. They used to put some traces on the horses to stop
them breaking into a gallop. If they did gallop they were
disqualified. There was betting on the races."

The Shows were not without their problems. It was resolved and
recorded in the Minute Book on 8 May 1935, "that the same man
that came in the show ground last year with a Fruit Stall is only
admitted this year on the understanding that he goes where he is
told by the Yard Steward." And, more seriously, on 22 November
1939 it was "proposed that in future we do not allow any swindlers
on the show ground".

Nevertheless, as Miss Bassett recalls, the Show was "a great social
event". To Mrs Hole it was

The prize-winners prepare to take their places in the Grand Parade.

"A place for meeting, a family show. I used to come back from the show and say I'd hardly seen any of it, because as soon as I entered the ground I met somebody and had a natter, you walked on, met somebody else."

The Women's Institute dispensed cups of tea and biscuits and provided chairs for the Band. The Minute Book records (June 21, 1933) that "The lowest tender was accepted for a band to play from 1 till 7 o'clock. In 1934 Ashover Band had this doubtful privelege.

It was a long, busy day and the band members would not be the only exhausted folk. For the farmers and their families the day began at 4 a.m. with milking. Then they were free to attend the show until it was time to go, as Mrs Hole says.

"We used to like to go and sit in the enclosure to watch the final cattle parade. And then we had to go back home to milk the cows again, so you couldn't stay too late."

Another agricultural and social event was the Ploughing Match. The matches took place on different "host" farms each year.

Ted Hellaby in his diary notes:
18 Oct 1931 Clay Cross Ploughing Match
26 Oct 1931 Ploughing stewards judged kale in Mellor field

Howard Davison enjoyed the challenge of these matches. He and his father used to put the plough on a cart and take it with perhaps one horse to wherever the ploughing match was. He would sometimes borrow another from the farm where the match was taking place. They couldn't travel a long way off but there were usually three matches yearly within reach, perhaps three or four miles away. He used to go to them every year and rarely came back without a prize of some sort.

"My father started me going to ploughing matches. And he'd stand and watch me and tell me what to do to perhaps make things look a bit better. And I got that I won quite a lot of prizes in my bit of ploughing time as well. There were no

The spectators perhaps making their own judgements in the Ploughing Match.

silver cups sent out to people in my ploughing days. It was just prize money that we won. – I did get one or two first prizes but generally, I was somewhere in the prize list, so I didn't do so bad, considering my plough wasn't the best of ploughs. Other people, they'd got better ploughs to work with and it sort of put me at a bit of a disadvantage. But I kept going and trying and competing.

They were busy days, for everybody. For folks who were staging the match on a particular farm, they'd be marking these fields out for competitors two or three days beforehand. Each plot had to be measured and marked out so that it was parallel with its next door neighbour and equal areas to be ploughed. And they'd have to put a stick up at either end of each plot and a number on it. And you'd draw for whatever number came up and you either got a good plot or a bad 'un then, because fields weren't always the same all over. There'd be perhaps rough patches and good patches and if you were unlucky you got a bad patch. The judges didn't allow for that. It was just your bad luck and you had to make the best of what you got.

When I used to go to ploughing matches, the aim then was to finish a very shallow furrow. You got your prize if you finished a good shallow furrow. And of course, it's only at ploughing matches that they finish furrows nowadays because in ordinary work on farms they have these reversible ploughs. You start at one side of the field, and you keep going till you get to the other side. And when you get to the end the plough's turned over and another set of ploughs turn the same direction going the other way, so all the land is turned over in one direction all the time and you've no riggs or furrows to worry about. But I'm not bothered with that. My idea is to plough the old traditional way. I get a lot of satisfaction out of setting these neat riggs and finishing these shallow furrows.

They judged you on whether you'd straight furrows, equal furrows. You hadn't got to have any uneven furrows. And no weeds or stubble showing; it'd got to be clean. And you'd got to have a levelling and a shallow furrow to finish off. And the general pattern of the work had got to be clean and tidy and neat. We should start soon after nine and you'd got to be finished by 2.30 p.m. Aye on local matches they did give and take a bit. If you'd not much to do at 2.30 p.m. they'd overlook it. If you'd a lot to do, I suppose they could disqualify you. Because, these ploughing matches, there was a lot of pottering about done on the ploughing. They'd not plough all the time. If there was a bit of a fault in the ploughing somewhere, they'd stop and shift it with their hands and push it into place and pull a bit of grass out that was showing. And when they were setting the rigg they'd go a yard or two – and move a bit of soil and go on a bit further and then they'd look back and they'd do a bit of something else to it. And it'd be just the same when they were finishing the furrow. They'd go a yard or two and then look back and if there was a bit of soil dropped in, they'd go back and push it out of the way with their hand. They were allowed to do that on local matches."

Henry Holmes remembers a significant event which was part of the Clay Cross Ploughing Match.

"I never ploughed with horses in a match, I did with tractors later on. And we used to do cutting hedges. But at the end of June, there used to be a scything competition. We used to hold it at Sharley Park, near where Jacksons lived. They used to give you a patch of ground and you had to scythe it, lay it in nice rows, cut it like a lawn and they used to judge them. I got a third for that one year and a mention on the radio. There could be up to teens of lads who'd enter. They'd be farm labourers from all round. That was quite an event."

As with the Ashover Show there were many events besides the ploughing. The catalogue for the Matlock Young Farmers' Ploughing Match held at Eddlestow Hall Farm in 1963 lists no less than 56 classes. Many weeks must have been spent, thinking and planning for such an occasion. There were thoughts too of the honour of winning prizes (which were monetary for all the classes except skittles where a bottle of whisky was awarded). There were classes for all kinds of preserves and cakes, embroidery and knitting. On the day there were "Competitions for stone walling" and "Tractor ploughing". As Howard says:

"There was a lot of stuff for ladies classes too. Even eggs, and in some cases there'd be turnips and mangolds. It was a miniature Ashover Show. Jam, lemon curd. Oh, it was a show for everybody. It was a very busy day – quite a full day for anybody to go and look round."

The advertisements included in the catalogue convey a sense of the time. H.A. Prince and Son of Kelstedge provided "Everything for the Farmer." J.H. Mudford and Sons Ltd. described themselves as "The Rope Men" and they were "Your local makers of stack sheets, wagon sheets, cart ropes off the shelf or made to measure." These were days when things were less disposable. They collected "old sacks in any condition" and resold these sacks "sound, cleaned and mended".

The ploughing matches and the agricultural show days, although they were hard work, were almost the only holidays for the farmers and their families.

Tossing the sheaf at Hearthstone Farm.

WOODTHORPE GRANGE

"I remember the wild flowers – purple violets in the hedgerow,
yellow rattle, meadow sweet, vetch, dog daises and heartsease,
scarlet poppies in the cornfields"

Woodthorpe Grange Farm is seen here through the eyes of
three different people. Before the second world war it was
worked by Ernest Smith. His daughter, Mrs Grace Else, describes
her young life there, evoking the variety and the quiet peaceful-
ness of those long ago days.

While Mr Smith farmed at Woodthorpe Grange a schoolboy,
Henry Holmes, spent all his spare time working on the farm. He

Woodthorpe Grange in Ernest Smith's time.

talks of the farm work which he really enjoyed.

In the late 1950s the Marriott family came to farm at Woodthorpe Grange. Colin Marriott talks about the farms his family worked as tenants at Temple Normanton and Williamthorpe as well as the arable and the dairy work at Woodthorpe Grange. His interest in the animals he cared for draws the reader into the story.

Grace Else writes:

Before the second World War, Woodthorpe was a quiet hamlet on the fringe of Ashover parish, consisting of a few farms and cottages. Woodthorpe Grange Farm was situated a mile from The Royal Oak Inn, Old Tupton, on the Ashover Road. Today much of that area has been taken over by housing on what used to be agricultural land, and the volume of traffic has increased.

It was quite common to meet people with a farm cart or horse drawn milk float. One such person was a farm worker with the name John Theodore Dye, always known as "Jack Dead", as he

A horse drawn milk float.

clattered down the road in a hurry. Another lady sat amongst her milk churns and measures as she returned from her round on the way home to Northedge. Then there was the timber drug, its haul drawn by three or four fine horses, going up Skelton's Hill en route to the timber yard of Allen and Orr, Chesterfield.

Ted Hellaby's diary:

2 November 1931 fetched ½ ton of oats from Bateman's Mill (6/8d)

Woodthorpe Mill existed for grinding farmers' corn. This was run by the Bateman brothers till the early 'thirties, when business ceased, the big wheel stopped turning, the water in the dam became silted up with mud and weeds and the mill stood empty and forlorn for some years. It is now a restaurant of note, still in the hands of the Bateman family.

Coldwell Farm was another near neighbour, owned by the Stone brothers. Their sister, Miss Clara Stone, was a skilled butter maker, always taking first prize at Ashover Show, her brothers gaining prizes with their sheep. At the foot of the farm lane was a spring of pure cold water used by nearby cottagers, passing travellers and in summer a milk churn kept its contents cool in the trough till collected by lorry. A reconnoitre in the 1970s revealed no trace of water anywhere!

We, at Woodthorpe Grange, kept cattle, pigs, a few sheep, poultry and two or three horses which played a major part in the land work, especially at harvest time. My father, Ernest Smith, would begin mowing very early in the morning at haytime, so that the horses would not be bothered by the heat or tormented by flies. Then followed swath turning, raking and piling into haycocks before finally leading the loads, roped onto the dray, back to the stackyard, where, with the aid of the picker they were built into stacks and later thatched with straw and pegs to keep out the rain.

Likewise, horses drew the binder when cutting the corn and carted the sheaves home in due course. In those fields I remember the wild flowers – purple violets in the hedgerow, yellow rattle, meadow sweet, vetch, dog daises and heartsease, scarlet pimpernels and poppies in the cornfields; the nests on the ground of lapwings, house martins under the eaves of the farmhouse and the cuckoo calling in Britton Wood.

The farmyard had ample buildings. Separated from the main yard by a gate, was the crew yard. Cattle could walk about freely, yet had shelter with access to feeding and the water troughs.

The Mixing Place had an earthy smell, for here a pulper, manipulated by hand, sliced turnips or mangolds to be mixed with cattle cake or meal, along with chopped straw. This was then shovelled into a skip (a wicker basket) and fed to the cows' mangers in the cowshed, where they

" Cuckoo "

A painting of Ted Hellaby's, dated 1 May 1986 records the cuckoo.

stood in pairs, separated by a wooden partition (we called it a boskin). Another door led outside to a mound in the orchard with a rusting remnant of an old gin race, a relic of corn grinding in the past.

The Stickplace held an assortment of small tools, rolls of barbed wire and logs ready to be chopped into sticks. I remember a road-man who, when working on his particular length or road, would bring his tea to be mashed at mid-day by my mother. He would sit on a stool in the Stickplace to eat his sandwiches and the bantam hens would be waiting to pick up the crumbs.

Threshing days occurred in Autumn and early Spring, with preparations beforehand, both outside and inside. Coal for the engine, sacks for carrying grain, a chamber cleared ready for storing corn and thatch removed from the stack, while in the kitchen a joint of meat cooked, potatoes were peeled, apple pies made, pears stewed and extra chairs hunted out.

Two threshing contractors lived locally, Bradleys and Nightingales. It was usually Harry Bradley who came to us. I can still see in my mind's eye the workers, each with his own job – the band cutter, another man feeding sheaves into the machine, corn carriers going up the steps to the chamber and the dusty job of carting away the chaff. I can still hear the hum of the drum. I can remember the excitement of our dogs and the hens picking among the leftovers at the end of the day.

1939 and war intervened. Farmers were urged to plough and sow all they could – and we had a new Fordson tractor on spade lugs. That was the beginning of a revolution in agriculture!

My father was a committee member of Ashover Show Society and helped before and after the event. He won prizes for roots. These were donated by the firm of Hadfield's Fertilizers. One prize, an EPNS teapot, had their name etched on the handle. As the Show coincided with Clay Cross wakes week they were days looked forward to with pleasure.

Many were the rambles to Ashover with my friends. We always stayed awhile at the Fabric Rock to admire the contrasting views – industrial one side, rural the other. Then, down many steps, under the two tunnels (the road above being the drive to Eastwood Grange), through fields to the village, ending at the Butts. A paddle in the Amber and sometimes tea at "Where the Rainbow Ends" café before walking home. There were also excursions to the Ashover Light Railway. We always looked to see which engine was pulling the carriages, as these were named after the Jackson

Grace Smith with her friends at a Sunday school treat at Woodthorpe Grange.

sisters and brothers.

Another walk was to the Mission Room at Alton for the whist drives. The room was lit by lamps, with warmth from a stove. Tea and sandwiches at half-time, then down a dark hill home, with only a pocket torch as a guide.

From the side door of Woodthorpe Grange I recall hearing the mellow sound of Ashover church bells ringing on Sunday mornings, coming from over the hill, and the rich scent of fruit, vegetables and flowers when we went to Harvest Festival at the same church.

Henry Holmes began working at Woodthorpe Grange Farm while he was still a schoolboy. He left school in 1933.

"I used to run home from school, to milk the cows at Woodthorpe Grange. It would be time for milking before I had my tea. The two chaps who worked there lived in the village, Press. They were older than me – they started me on the farming. I never wanted to be a farmer, although I worked on farms for 25 years, but it was love of animals really.

We milked about 25 cows on average, at Woodthorpe. There was the boss, Mr Smith, and his son Arthur. I enjoyed the hand milking. My father used to come on the farm when it was hay time and help us. He was retired from the mine. He came in one day when we were milking and I sat him down under one of the cows. And he milked, as though he'd been doing it daily – you never forget it once you've done it. I learnt to milk before I left school.

When a cow is newly calved, she'll probably give four gallons of milk and then as the lactation goes on, she gradually gives less, because it's meant for the calf. And it ends up with her giving a pint, but you don't stop milking them, because in warm weather, the milk is liable to curdle and they get mastitis, so you keep milking them as long as you can. Well, they used to give me what they called the "strippers". "Shall you strip that one out?" And the boss came in one day and he said, "Which has Henry milked?" He went round them all and he found they were clean (and I was only a school lad then) and he never tried again. But it was seven days a week, twice a day. And at one time he was selling a lot of his milk to a man, Harry Mason, who had a milk round in Clay Cross. He used to like to get his milk so he could get round the houses and that meant we had to get up earlier and earlier. He'd come into the cowshed and put it through the cooler and get a churn full and off he'd go with that and deliver it and come back for the rest, he was so keen. Of course, we were working till nearly seven o'clock every night and there was no time off."

There was arable work to be done too.

"Woodthorpe Grange Farm was about 120 acres. Until about 1938 we did it all with horses. I used to mow at least 50 acres every year with horses. There was three eight acre fields and we used to cut them in two. Mow bottom half and then the top half. And I always remember – I was mowing in this big eight acre field and there was a German war plane came over. I think he'd fired his guns at Matlock somewhere near the cinema and he was hedge-hopping and he came straight over the field where I was. I didn't realise it till afterwards.

I enjoyed working with the horses. He bought a horse from a farm in Lea and he took me over to fetch it, from Lea to Woodthorpe. And I rode him bareback. He was a cart horse actually, and I rode him bareback from Lea back down to Woodthorpe and that was a great experience. But in those days, they used to have drovers. They used to stand in the market (Bakewell, for example) and if a farmer bought a cow and it was within ten miles of Bakewell market, they used to drive it home for him. And they would come through Matlock. You can't believe it now, can you?

Arthur Smith was two years younger than me. His uncle lived in Lea and he bought him a donkey from a farm at Holloway and two young bulls. And we walked them from Holloway to Woodthorpe three of us. We came down through Carr Woods and the walls were down at each side and however we did it, I don't know. But we'd got the donkey and every time you got on him, to ride him, he came round and went the other way, backwards. But we got them there and Arthur had this donkey for about three years.

Between 14 and 17, I developed a lot and grew. I remember going to Ashover Show the first year I left school. There was a man guessing your weight and if he didn't guess it, he'd give you a few coppers back. He guessed me at six stone one and I was six stone four, so I was not very heavy. I learned to plough with horses, and when you get to the end, you've got to wheedle the plough round and I wasn't up to that, for a start. But the hydraulic lift revolutionised farming. But the horses knew what to do. You've got the lines, to steer them but you don't really need them because the horse knows exactly what to do. As an instance, we used to lead all the manure from the cowsheds up into the fields and pull it out in heaps. Some of the fields were quite steep. I used to go with a load, leading the horse, and I gave him a rest when it was on the collar (when you were going up hill). You only had to do it once, but the next time you went with a load, he'd stop in exactly in the same place.

And the cows too had their particular ways. When you're fetching them from the pasture fields, when they're getting nearer to the bottom, they'll all form one single line and it's the same cows in the front all the time and the stragglers behind. They tell me that it goes back to the days when fields weren't cultivated. It was woodland and there were paths. And in old pasture fields you still see cow paths, although they've no need of them.

When I got to about 20 I was called up for the Army and I passed out and everything. But meanwhile (I was in a reserved occupation) the people I worked for got me off. I was actually called up and I got to the point of going round my friends and relatives saying "Cheerio" and then this letter came through that I was reprieved. I was hurt really because most of my mates went into the Army. But it was a good thing for me, because I'd hardly been out of the village. I wasn't worldly-wise. That's when I went back to the Church. I used to milk on Sunday mornings and I used to walk from Press to Ashover Church and get back for lunchtime – walk over the Fabric. I did that for several years."

Farm work may have seemed a safer option but was not without tragedy.

"My uncle farmed Tinkley Lane farm for his uncle. One particular day he was going into the field. (Before they had muck spreaders they used to pull the manure out in heaps and then go with a fork and spread it. He was going to Tinkley

Lane to one of the fields to do some muck spreading.) Bailey's corn lorry had delivered some bags of corn and he was going the same way. My uncle jumped on the step of the lorry and rode on the side with the fork under his arm. When they got to the field, he hopped off and the lorry carried on, but it went over him and killed him."

Ted Hellaby's diary:

18 March 1931. Fetched oats from Bateman's Mill. 6s.8d. for 80 stone @ 1d. per stone. Took 53 stone more to be ground.

Mrs Else remembered Bateman's Mill, but it was more interesting for a boy. As a schoolboy, Henry Holmes used to

"go to Bateman's Mill and there was a nice orchard across the road. Polly Bateman used to wear either a bonnet or a man's cap, with long clothes on and quite stout she was. You'd go to the house for a pennyworth of apples and she'd come to the door with 'em in her cap. There'd be seven or eight for a penny. There was a dam and we always ran to look over the wall. You'd see the water voles. Late the farmer that I worked for used to take a cartload of grain down and have it ground for feeding the cows. It was a dusty place."

Colin Marriott enjoyed milking as a little boy at Temple Normanton.

"Oh I bet I were no more than eight or nine. I used to milk with me Dad and me older brother. I used to have a little bucket and a stool. Then, they'd go round and try it after I'd done and see if I'd cleaned it all out. The men used to have to go like that, see, (use just forefingers and thumb) because the tits weren't big enough. But I could go better with them, because I had small hands. I was quite good at milking, right from being a little lad. In fact two of the neighbours used to come round to watch me milk. They said I was so good, I were only little and I couldn't half belt it out. I suppose they used to pick quiet uns for me, because they're not all calm, kind, cows aren't. They can be rough.

We started with a milk round. Me dad never took to driving but me mother picked it up straight away. We had this new van and it come from Kennings at Clay Cross. (Funnily enough, the young chap as delivered it, got to stop to show 'em how to go on with it – I suppose it was "Tell me this and tell me....." – were my future wife, Georgie's, uncle.) We used to get up every morning and do milking, then put churns in the back of this van and take 'em. But if something went wrong with that, we used to put pony in the float and trot off. At first we used to take the milk to Heath, it weren't far to Heath Station through Holmewood, and put it on train there. There'd be the one churn, 15 gallons. Then we used to come back, have us breakfast and go to school. And me mother, she had a milk round then, used to put this milk churn in back of van and go round houses up to Sutton Scarsdale.

Then, as my brother got older he got more cows and he said "You've got another man wants some milk, Ibbotsons at Sheffield." We used to bring that milk down to Clay Cross Station for the Midland Railway line. First we used to go to Heath, leave that churn there for porter to carry, and then come shooting down to Clay Cross. That train left Clay Cross at two minutes to seven. She used to do that every morning, me mother. She did it for years. Then things altered.

We was milking between 20 and 30 cows. There was three of us to do it, me and me brother and me dad. We didn't have a farm lad, but when I got to 17 I started driving lessons and got me driving licence. We'd got a Vauxhall car then, one of

Clay Cross Station.

them big ones – we used to put churn in there. And then, we stopped fetching milk to the station. They stopped all that when Milk Board come and then a lorry used to pick it up and we'd put a ticket on where it were going, then they'd send the money through bank. We still had milk round, but you had to pay a levy on it to Milk Board.

When you milk by hand, idea is to squeeze and pull a bit – let your hand go, it comes in to tit again. Same as milking machine. It sucks, stops sucking, sucks. It has to stop sucking and let go just enough to hold cluster on, so that milk'll come down into tit. If it held it all time, it wouldn't milk. Same as a calf, when he sucks, he goes like that, doesn't he? (Here he makes a lovely sucking shape with his mouth and imitates the noise.) Then while he's swallowing it, some more milk runs into tit. And if it doesn't, he starts butting it, because he's not getting enough. Same with lambs, I don't know about babies because I've never suckled one! Oh ah, I can remember the noise, till bucket-bottom got full, then as it went on you just heard squatting on top of milk. Then it used to all froth up. But now, oh, it's entirely different altogether now, milking is, from what it was.

There were siles to filter the milk. The sile was a big round stainless steel dish. You put a small gauze in bottom, then a paper filter over top of that, and that had a clip on it. Clover Leaf they called it. (That were the make you wanted.) Then you put a bigger filter on top and you put a spring clip on that, so it didn't come out. Then if your milk were middling, going through a bit too slow, you used to take it out, wash it all out and put another in, because that'd happen done its time, filtered too many. It would stop cleaning, well it wouldn't go through fast enough for you.

Then we started with a machine. We used to have a bucket with four clusters on and a stationary engine in barn. And you started it up – there were a pipe line right down top o' cow-shed with a vacuum. You put your pipe on each one and carried it from one cow to the next. The cows took to that easily. It weren't long after we'd had machine, that they wouldn't let you hand milk again. If you sat under one, they'd kick you straight away. For a start, they used to kick bucket. New calved ones were the best, when they'd just calved. Oh, ah, they're rough things cows. Ah, times many I've had a bucket tipped over. I've had them big milking machines kicked over, them buckets with the clusters on. Ah some of them – I don't know what'd make 'em do it.

All our milk cows had names, they did, ah. They were all pedigree cows, registered in a book, and all milk they gave every week was recorded. And oh, they'd all got – names, "Fill-pail". "Fill-pail the second" and "Molly" and all kinds of names, anything we could think of. Ah, they all 'ad names, cows, whether they knew it, I don't know, but we used to have to know 'em. And now, they don't, see. They're all ear-tagged, numbered and branded on their hind quarters. So you look round for this number. And if one of our bulls or beasts goes to market, you have to go through 'em all in case one's lost its number. If it's not got a number in you daren't send it. And every one has a little book – a passport. It's a little book now. At one time, you'd have a chart to take 'em to market with all lot on it. If they'd got one tag in, they'd be all right, but now they've got to have two. They've got to be tagged when they're calves so you can tell which mother they've come off. (That's all started from foot and mouth.) And them foreigners don't want our meat, because we're not strict enough for them! I don't know what's going to happen to job.

They didn't used to have the big ear tags. No, no. Used to have little silver tags in cows. I can't think what brought that in. It didn't matter if it were going to be slaughtered. But if you had a pedigree herd – Friesians, Ayrshires, whatever it was – a bloke used to come and record you every so many weeks, weigh 'em, see you were doing your job right. He'd put 'em all down in a big book. They used to tattoo 'em. They'd stamp it in their ears. That number stopped forever. That were for pedigree you see. And then when the calf's born, within a few weeks you have to paint this picture of it. You have a book, and where the calf has a black pattern, you black that in and where it's white you leave it. Make that picture in that book look like that cow. You can see then it follows its mother and father for pedigree. They've always done that with pedigrees. If you were buying a new heifer, you'd want to know that cow's mother, how much milk it's given, how much her mother's given. How many gallons she's given each lactation. That goes all through, for recording for your pedigrees.... Without the herd book you could say any calf's off of that cow. But you can't, see, because you've already recorded it when it's a few days old. You keep the book till you sell the cow."

In the days when regulations were more relaxed, Mr Marriott took his small children into the cowshed with him.

"Oh I used to feed ours many a time with bottle, to give missus a rest. When our Roger were little, I used to put him in pram, push him up into cowshed and he'd sit there watching me and he'd have his bottle with some milk in. And he chucked it out once. I thought "Oh, he wants some more". Took teat off, squirted some in – ooh, he was happy as owt with that. And as Sandra came, and she got older, Georgie, my wife, used to put her in push chair and bring her up. It would give her a break from 'em for a bit. Kids liked it. They loved it, watching me running about with buckets and milk and cows, because it were clean in shed. Sandra used to be same. You'd bring her a little bottle, she'd suck away. They were lovely kids, I used to get teat off, just squirt 'em a drop more in, pass it to 'em and that pacified them a bit longer. Oh we had a happy life. But I don't suppose you're supposed to do it straight from cow like that now."

Conditions for the cows have improved in one way.

"The flies used to bother them, but we don't have so many flies now because this last few years, they've got different stuff out – pour it on cow's back, they'll have no flies settle on them. And the flies'll not go in that shed when they've been in with that, for many a while. The flies 'll not pester cows like they used to do. They'll only fly round top of 'em, not settle on them. They don't like smell of that. At one time, we used to buy fly spray. Keep spraying 'em. That used to roll 'em over, but it wasn't as powerful as this."

But even with modern methods there is still opportunity for the farmer who enjoys his animals as individuals.

"Things have changed, of course and it's all AI now. (You get some good calves. These 'ere people that produce semen, they only use best bulls.) We've got two cows and calves in another shed. And there's one, he doesn't want to suck enough off mother. I take some milk in a bucket and he comes running up to me and he drinks some out of a bucket, that one. Them others don't bother but that one looks forward to it now, so I've got to keep going up twice a day with a bucket. It's no trouble. These others with long trough. I pour it in long trough: ooh, you ought to see 'em, they're going mad to get stuck in. Then other side, they're all in pens. If they are too small though, they come through them bars on their own."

Milk was – or might be – different at one time.

"It were when roots were being harvested, cabbage and one thing and another. All at once our Roger started with tummy ache in night. No sleep. So I said, "I know what it is, we've started using cabbage and it's upsetting his stomach." I said, "see that cow stood on her own at bottom?" I says, "Don't give her no more." Give her corn and hay. Within two days, he'd never a bit more belly-ache. He went on perfect just because she were having corn and hay. Milk must have been better for him. And when I was delivering milk, I used to laugh at these women. When I walked in door they'd say, "You're giving them cows too many turnips." They used to play hell. "Our so and so has been up all night with stomach ache." "Oh." I says, "I'm sorry. We'll cut 'em off a bit then". They did, you know, these women did."

Delivering the milk was different too, and not always pleasant.

"We used to take it in a bucket then. Ah, pour it into jug or basin. These were big buckets with a rack inside. You could hang the measure on. It was a half pint measure. They were tin buckets and cold to hands, ah, because you couldn't wear gloves. You'd have to take 'em off to measure it in. Bottles are easier and quicker, but you've got to bottle before you set off. And we used to have some cold winters at that time of day. It were all cold everywhere, on farms them days."

Another important part of the farm was work with the sheep.

"Right from me being a little tiny kid, me dad always had a few sheep. Used to have a few lambs early on in spring. I've

Feb. 23rd 1976.   Springtime

always messed with sheep. Do what wanted doing. During lambing time, used to look after them a bit."

Ted Hellaby's diary:
> 5 March 1931 First lamb arrived today (Ewe lamb.) Got chop place ready today for lambs.
> 6/7 March Little short ewe lambed this afternoon.
> 16 March Another ewe very bad but improving tonight.
> 17 March Ewe improving.
> 18 March Ewe nearly right.
> 25 April Last ewe lambed (tup lamb.)

"Then, when they got older, used to turn 'em into field and that were it. Go round 'em every day, watch 'em and when they wanted docking tails and castrating and that a friend used to come and do that for us. Same with clipping, he always used to clip 'em after we had 'em dipped. Used to do his own, then come up with clippers. They were portable clippers. They used to fold up into a bag to carry. It were like a three-legged trolley. There was a gear system on top. We turned handle, and that worked down and worked his clippers. I should turn one, me brother he'd turn next, to make clippers go. He used to clip like mad. They all had 'em on big farms because they used to clip horses with 'em for winter, take all long hair off. I can see it now, clipping 'em off, turning handle."

The sheep needed constant attention and looking over.

Ted Hellaby's diary:

December 1st 1931. Dressed ewes feet and dosed them.

"If you kept sheep, you had to go to Police Station twice a year at least because them sheep had to be dipped. You had to notify what date you were going to do 'em at and time. You filled in a form – we used to go to Chesterfield with ours, – I suppose we could have gone to Clay Cross. You'd have to state what time you were going to start dipping, then you'd notified bobby. That was the main thing. Then, ten-to-one, they'd send a policeman to watch you doing 'em. He'd either come round on his bike, or if he didn't want to come, he didn't. And he'd stand at end if he were a bit keen and time 'em. They had to be in that dip for so long. And then all at once they said, "Oh, we're not bothered about that. You don't have to do them." Because it were their idea to dip them sheep. So, if anybody had a mishap, through breathing this or getting it on their skin and it made 'em bad, they were responsible you see. So was them as made dips. I know one or two that been bad with them .... but they say they've never been able to claim.

We used to wear leg slips and that sort of stuff. We'd got a little portable dip, we managed with that for years. Used to put it on trailer, take it to them fields at Holmewood there. Take digger or spade and dig hole. Drop it in it and connect a pipe up to trough. We'd put it in a fenced field near a trough and you'd have to be filling it up all time you were dipping, so much gets used up, keep putting a bit of fresh dip in. Used to send 'em out of this dip on to a long sheet of tin for draining back. You'd have a little gate at end and when they'd had time to drain off, they'd jump off into field. Then we got a proper big dip. We used to empty it all out, then start with fresh. We'd have a big pen. Drive 'em all into a big pen, keep pushing 'em through into a little pen, so you could get hold of them, chucking them in. They hate it but it were good for them, dipping. I mean, look at Chatsworth, used to dip theirs several times a year to keep flies and that off them. They were always pushing 'em in. Some people would have a pole to push them in with. What I did, I made a piece of wood, bored hole in it and put shaft in it and nailed it through and used to turn 'em over, like that. But if Bobby didn't come, you didn't bother, just push 'em through. Properly though, you were meant to push the sheep under the water. Cover all their body up and put their heads under once. 'Cause they were deep, you know, them dips. Four foot deep, they hold some water, and the sheep will float on top. We'd no drainers up there, they didn't put one in. So to empty it we used to get a big hosepipe, biggish bore like. Turn on tap at one end, hold it up other end, fill it up to top. One of us hold it up, take it right down to dip when we wanted to empty it. Drop that end in

A portable sheep dip at Hilltop Farm.

there, run down field with other end. It used to empty itself, siphon it off.

You used to have to use sheep seal dip once a year. That were rum stuff, special for delousing. Louse, you see, take some killing. If you had a sheep in market which had got sheep scab on it, they'd play hell with you. You used to have to report that to police. If you had an outbreak you had to gather them all in then, didn't matter what time of year it was, lambing time or what, all had to be gathered in and dipped. I've see 'em do it when they've been close to lambing. If you bought some out o' market with that sheep scab, they

Bakewell Market

were ever so strict. They don't bother now though. Just how things have altered all at once. Before that, if you'd bought a few sheep and you hadn't got a licence with them, they'd not been dipped. And they came round (the men from the Ministry) "You've not dipped these," and straight away you had to get shot on 'em. If you bought some store lambs out o'market (we used to buy quite a lot of store lambs, we breed us own now, but we didn't for a few years) they'd be catalogued, saying where they were from and everything.

Ted Hellaby's diary:

  24 September 1931 Bought 11 single theives¹ and 1 ram off F.
  Bennett for £34.16s.0d.

If you know whose they were you'd fancy buying 'em. It would say on them when they were last dipped. If you'd got a paper

---

¹ Theives are ewes of the first or second year that have not yet borne a lamb.

from sales, that these sheep had all been dipped they were already done for you so many weeks. Also, if they'd been wormed, drenched and all them sort of things. (It's the same with cattle, isn't it?) Now they're strict and every lamb's got to be numbered. All them lambs now, you cannot take them to market, without your serial number on. You buy your numbers and they'll not sell a sheep without a number in its tab. That's since foot and mouth. They know where everything is in country.

Then there were the pigs, we always had a pig. Then when we got to Williamthorpe, we had more space there, we had rather a lot of pigs, me and me brother.

In a litter of pigs we used to reckon to rear eight or nine. Seven were all right, but you weren't very pleased if you only reared seven. Best litter we ever had was when we first came up here. And there were four very little pigs. Georgie and our Sandra used to put 'em in back of car, (because she used to come up and clean house for a long while before we came to live here and I used to work out in fields). Used to bring these four little pigs and give 'em a bit of what you call "Sow-lac" stuff a time or two a day. And then when we went back at night we used to put 'em in shed with others. That sow reared 16, that litter. She had 16 pigs and she reared every one, sow did. We brought em up here.

What we used to do, if one had a big litter and some of them were small, we used to get a little tin, put it at back where sow couldn't get at it, pour 'em a drop in. And they weren't long before they were supping it up like that. I don't know what it was, I never asked. We used to call it Sow-lac, I suppose because sow were lacking milk. But ah, they used to do ever so well on it. Then as they got bigger, you used to buy little pellets, they used to chew them up. Oh we used to spend a bit of time with pigs and they used to grow well. They're interesting, though, pigs are. At one time here we had ten breeding sows, we'd no room for any more. But father-in-law thought cows would be better so when we had bits of trouble with one or two, we didn't bother and we cut 'em down. Turned buildings into where we put calves.

We used to have us own boar at one time. If we didn't, we used to take 'em to where there were one when sow were on heat. I've been known to walk 'em up field. Funnily enough, you drive pig up to that boar and when she's got served and comes back, she'll come straight back home on her own, through gap she's gone through nearly. Their sense of smell is good, they know their own road back. Ah, they're no trouble. They always seemed to come back all right. Harry Abbott used to keep a good boar pig down at Handley Lane there.

We had a lot of fowl when we first came up here in 1959. I bought a shed and we had it put down that field, through kitchen door there. We had a hundred pullets in it. And then, we had two little sheds in stack yard with some more hens in and there were folks coming all time for eggs. We did ever so well with 'em. And egg-man, he used to come round and clean us up every week. What we hadn't sold to milkmen – these milkmen used to come and buy 'em every so many days. Then we had 'em up in loft and of course when the corn was harvested, we had to take 'em out of loft. You see, you want to store corn up there. After threshing day, when we'd the corn bagged up, we used to have all hens in loft.

For some farmwork we'd still got horses. There was still a sale for a horse that could work. I broke one in for father-in-law. They had it running about the fields a long while and didn't bother with it. I kept pulling their leg, saying "'bout time you did something with that filly", so one day she says, "You take it then, get it going". I thought, "I've done summat now." I went up and fetched it. It went on a treat. She were a beauty, she were. We used to talk to them like humans. Some were a lot better than others. Some were always a bit thick. But also, I used to like riding. Used to be a chap that we knew, that used to buy little ponies from pits, he used to leave us one or two, to quieten them down and, as we got older, we bought one, a good 'un for ourselves. He used to go to Wales and all round, buy a lot of 'em. Very often he'd pick a nice one and he'd say, "You can have this one for a month or two and ride it". And he'd get a good price for it, when it was quieter, ride it and put it in float.

Best way to break a horse in was to take him in a morning, then you wouldn't take him in afternoon. It would be too much for him. You could spoil one. Then after a few weeks, you'd got his legs, his mouth and all his limbs hard, then you could take him a full day, but it'd be too much for him, the first six months, something like that. You could do it with the help of an older one. Aye, tie him to side of it. But if you'd got one that were a bit flirty, you'd get him quietened down in yard on a rope, till he'd get to know what you're talking about. That were main thing, train 'em properly, make a nice quiet horse. The more you played with him, the better he got. Then you wouldn't put him in shafts, carts and that for a while, till he got really used to everything. That were another shock

August 25ᵀᴴ 1977.

to them, they could try to take off, do all sorts then. When he got used to being worked, used to being touched, then you'd put him in cart. You backed him in. See, you'd tip cart up, like that, that's how they used to do it, stand it up, then you'd back him in, you'd pull it down steady just drop him on, put shafts down side and chain him into thing with chains. You were always better to have one or two lads with you, very handy in case he started playing up.

They all had names, straight away. Oh, aye I've done quite a lot with horses, me and me brother. Everything, cutting corn and mowing grass with a hay rake, leading loads in. We used to do a lot with horses. In fact, I like horses. Me brother did as well. We'd some good ones. We used to enjoy it. We used to have nice Sunday times before the war. Some of my brother's mates used to come, and we'd go to different farms a Sundays. We used to ride 'em down field in us turns. Sometimes, dinner time, when we come home from school, one or two'd come up from school and have a ride round field on one of our horses. Oh, ah, we used to saddle 'em as we got older as well."

It was harder work than using a tractor, but more rewarding.
"Of course, you couldn't get as much done. There was a lot you could do with 'em but then you'd got to put more work into it, feeding 'em and looking after 'em, clipping their throat, their bellies, so far up. It would keep them cleaner and stop them sweating so much when they were working. Because they was inside, in a stable in winter. They didn't go out till summer. It automatically goes off a horse in summer time. He only has a very fine coat, see he's lost all his warm hair. Same as cows, they always have a winter coat, but if horses keep that on, they get sweaty .... sometimes we used to keep 'em clean without combing and brushing 'em, pull the hair off before it grew long – if we fetched em in early enough."

Life was easier in lots of ways when a tractor was acquired.
"I can remember having my first tractor, plain as owt. A Fordson. After me dad died, me mother lost all her nerve and she couldn't drive no more and I used to take her. And – I think it were about 1940 – we was going on Vicar Lane. There were Kennings, just a show room and a garage there. You could buy cars on there. But this new tractor was stood on this lorry. Just what we wanted. I said, "That's what we want. Can't keep pace with horses, tires 'em out too much. It's one of them that we want." "Yes we do." says mother. So we walked into – I couldn't believe it – walked into garage, looked round this tractor. She wants to go in office and have a word with him. So he says, "Well I'll tell you price and everything about it and I'll send the Clay Cross man, Calladine, up, see what he says. (Because we'd already had dealings with him.) So he put this tractor on lorry and brought it to our house. First tractor. And I can tell you how much it cost. It cost £195. Ah, it had big mudguards on, to protect on front, they were ever so nice. It didn't have a cab. Oh no, cabs, didn't come in for a long while. We had one with lights on and starter on before cabs come in. And it had no lights at all. They were years before they put lights on 'em because war were going, you wouldn't be able to go and work in the fields you see with

lights. Used to go in when moon was shining, go and do a bit.

We'd got two more after a bit, we'd got one of them big Ingham tractors. We were first to have one of them. Me brother, he used to drive this old 'un a bit. We'd had that first tractor about four years – we'd had engine done up. One day this bloke come round to me brother, wanting to buy it. So when I come in at night with mine, this chap who were working for us says to me, "I've sold tractor today." So I says, (sarcastically) "Ah, I shouldn't be surprised at that." (because generally it hadn't been looked after.) "Oh," he says, "he give me a good price for it." – And we'd had it all that while, tyres were about worn on it, but he'd given him £300 for it. All work it did, and this chap come and give us all that more than we paid. So it just shows things were starting to go up. Ah, we had ploughs, cultivators, discs, tractor corn drills and everything. The only disadvantage was that it was cold doing field work with tractors, terrible cold things, tractors. Now, they're marvellous now. They're warmer than in! In fact, they're better than most cars."

The constant round of work included cleaning the hedge bottoms.
"Before you ploughed, when you'd mowed a field of hay, all grass left in hedge bottom, cows went to graze there and they'd eat that off. They always kept that nice. At one time you'd clean the hedge bottom out by hand. They don't now because they've got hedge cutters and then these sprays, they kill it, stop it growing. But all hedges were done by hand when we first came here. Used to clean ditches out with shovels. Then we bought a thing to put at back of tractor. That scooped 'em out. Now you've got massive big gear."

As the year went on hay making time came.
"Oh ah, we used to rake it up, cock it all up into heaps and then hay cocks like, go round with fork, lift it up, put it on drays. And then, me and me brother, we bought this second-hand hay loader. A lot of farmers already had one afore us. Just tie it to back of trailer and it'd pick it up, push it up on trailer – that were a great help. Then we had a picking pole, it lifted hay onto stack. That was a big pole, you reared him on side of stack, with about four ropes, then it'd got a bar

across and you used to pull it down onto a wire rope, shove this big fork in load and pull this catch up – these two forks went across. Used to have horse and tell him to pull it up, pull this wire up and it used to swing it round on top of stack. Coo, it'd empty a load in about three sticks. If you wanted, you could pull it up with a car or anything, but we used to do it with the horse."

Later in the year came harvest time.

"Harvest used to be a rough job because it were all hard work. We used to cut it, put it into sheaves, stook 'em all up while they dried, cart 'em in. It was rough on your arms. But you got used to it, ah, if there were no thistles it were all right. We'd be working long hours but we used to pack up when it went damp. If you were leading sheaves or hay and it was one of them sort of nights when the dew came down earlier and crop went damp, you'd have to leave it then, because it were no good if you led it 'cause it'd get warm."

Then we made the stacks. Made some lovely haystacks and I thatched them. We used to put a bit of a peg on and sometimes put a bobbin on top of it to finish it off. I like thatching, I do. It's really simple, when you get to do a bit. The worst job's making the roof nice to put thatch on. You straighten it all out and make a long roll of straw, tie it up. That's what they call a rig bat. See, that makes it go pointed. When you're thatching a corn stack, your sheaves, you can't get them pointed like that. They're

A farm lad is leading the horse forward to work the picker.

just flat, so you put this bat of straw down top. Peg that on, then, when you put your thatch up, it goes up over top and that supports it. It has to come over other one so much. Same as roofing tiles, they all have to overlap. You put the rigbat on as you go. Or you can please yourself. You can put one right down top first and then if your stack's not very good at bottom, you put another one right across bottom to hold your thatch on. You get your straw, lay it down in overlapping layers, along the length of the stack. You call 'em welts. You make sure the overlapping layers are all nice and level. See, when rain comes, it just hits straw at the top (over the rigbat) and it runs right down off to floor without going into stack. You put your straw in layers, because corn's not very long straw. A big stack'd happen have about seven of these, then all rows of string across, pegging it on, just to keep wind from blowing it off. It's quite interesting, thatching is. I used to like it although you'd got to walk up and down ladder. You tried to get someone to give you a hand, carry some up, get pegs – another job, we used to have to find pegs.

You used to have to make the pegs if you run out, but sometimes you could buy 'em. Then, you'd take 'em off every year, if you took 'em off right you saved 'em, sharpen some of 'em sometimes. Sometimes there'd be square uns, all sorts, whatever you could buy. Used to take a lot you see, because there were all the stacks.

There's a proper way of putting pegs in. You don't shove peg in like that (pointing into the stack) because water'd follow it in. You shove it up,

Thatching a stack,
Henry Holmes is on the ladder.

straight across like that. Wind didn't blow it so bad, so then water, coming down, when it hit that peg, didn't go through into stack, it'd run off. Sometimes, if we couldn't get thatch on soon enough, if you couldn't get a chance to get it on while it waited for thrashing, all of top of stack wouldn't be very good, water'd soak in. But if you got 'em all thatched down, rain never went in. Quite good, successful job that is, thatching. And then, last two stacks we had here, before combine had got going properly, they started making great big polythene sheets. Then we used to buy a big long net, roll sheet on – cover a stack up in no time and roll these nets on, tie them or peg 'em down and stack were covered up. Whereas it used to take a long while to thatch one.

We used to have a haystack at Williamthorpe that were always showing up to lane and we used to put a round end on that one. Make it look nice, go round on t'other side. You just come round with it, press it in a bit as you're making it, if you're going to thatch end, you have it leading in a bit. See, keep coming round with your straw, peg it in till you got so you could go down other side. There's some folks used to thatch ends regular. Kept wind from blowing in ends for one thing. Bit of a slow job, but it used to look nice when ends were thatched. There wasn't much we couldn't do. You've got to do, haven't you, in farming? My son, there's not much he can't do in repair jobs. I were never very brilliant at repairs. I used to get somebody else to do it. I never fancied repairing, but anything else I could do."

When there was a suitable time, the corn had to be threshed.

"We used to have a threshing machine, me and me brother, when we were up at Williamthorpe. It were one day when we couldn't get nobody to thrash it. He heard of this one for sale, so he went and bought it cheap. And we bought a baler. A wooden threshing drum, they were good they were. Turn it into stackyard and tractor used to drive it from a belt. First off steam man used to come round. Then when we got a tractor, he didn't use his steam engine, he used to use our tractor. Save buying coal. I remember when the steam one came round. Ah, it were a busy day, carrying water, I've had hours and hours carrying water for that thing when I were a

kid. Two of you. Then you couldn't satisfy it. And coal – no end
of coal. Used to be a gang of men on. It were a nice noise, used
to go softly, chuff-chuff, and then drum was drrrrr all the
time. Same as when we started with tractor, you could hear
that purring away and drum buzzing away. We were lucky,
where we lived, It were near pit, near chaps. We used to go
and get fixed up with some men. "We're going to thresh stack
this weekend." – Most of the miners had been farming, then
for some unknown reason they'd gone down pits. There
weren't many miners couldn't do farm work. Especially in
harvest, going round picking sheaves, chuck 'em on trailers
and then emptying 'em on stacks. In fact, we had two used to
come, when we started leading sheaves. Same two of 'em used
to come, one used to go on stack with me, pass 'em to me,
other one chucking 'em on as fast as ……….. They'd come
with trailer and go back for another load. He'd have it
emptied on to stack. That were going right till dark: they used
to knock off work in the mine early, because they started
early. And all they wanted were to scrape trailer bottom up,
when they'd took sheaves off – scrape it all off and put it in a
bag – get as much of that as they could. Take it to shed on
allotment for their fowls. They could get enough to last them
for a long while. There was method to their madness, same as
they'd have muck for their allotments. Oh ah, they were ever
so good."

THE FARM ACCOUNTS

Bills and receipts tell a great deal about the everyday working of a farm. This chapter looks at two separate lots of accounts which run almost concurrently. The account book of Bernard Brailsford, who was the farm manager for John Bassett at Hilltop Farm in Ashover, has survived. It is in the form of a foolscap size ledger and shows "accounts paid" on the left hand page and "accounts received" on the right hand. It contains a single entry for 1920, but from 1922 – 1938 it is complete.

A quite different system was used by Bernard Davison who owned Dale Bank Farm, Milltown. He bought the farm in 1925 having moved from Demonsdale Farm. Bills and receipts were pushed onto metal spikes made from fence wire in the order in which they were received. The bills have been undisturbed and so preserved. One of the spikes held the accounts for the years 1924 – 1939, although there was not a complete set for each year. These include the household accounts but only those relating to the farm have been examined. Once they had been slowly and carefully extricated from the spike on which they had resided for so long, it was found that they had gathered some of its rust and many were fragile and, in parts, illegible but generally they have survived well.

Hilltop Farm comprised about 120 acres. Dale Bank Farm had grown by the 1930's to 60 acres. This difference in size is reflected in the accounts. Those for Hilltop Farm specify both items bought and goods and services sold, whereas Dale Bank's accounts are generally bills to pay. For the years 1925 – 1929, (until 1927 Mr Davison was at Demonsdale Farm) however, receipts from the Ashover Light Railway show that Mr Davison was transporting milk for sale. In 1938 the Milk Marketing Board was established, so they would take the milk and from that period there are bills for bottles and bottle caps, because the farm was also supplying bottled milk for a relative's Tupton milk round. Perhaps the size of Dale Bank Farm meant that it was important to account very carefully for money that was spent. The accounts are fuller than those for Hilltop Farm.

From the years covered by both sets of accounts 1934 is the year which has been examined, for it is the one where both sets are complete. Although, they worked on different systems, a number of interesting similarities and differences can be seen. Whilst those for Hilltop are clearly set out, for Dale Bank, the relevant bills needed to be selected and itemised, so that the two could be compared month by month. 1934 came between two contrasting years for weather. 1933 had been "an exceptionally dry year" (after a fairly wet spring with, in late February, "heavy snow .... great drifts.") and "sunshine records had been the best of the century (except for 1911)." Temperatures between June and September had been "well above normal". In fact that period had been "the warmest since before 1881". December though was "the coldest since 1890 in much of England and Wales". In 1934, after a wet spring "June, July and September were exceptionally warm" and, in contrast to the previous year, "December was the warmest for over 60 years". In May 1935 there was "a heavy snowfall, with severe cold", but late June to mid-August "was unusually warm, sunny and very dry". The wet springs and warm summer months meant that in 1933 and 1934 there was an exceptionally good crop of wheat and the yield was "above average" for 1935. In fact, generally "all crops flourished" in 1934. (Information from J.M. Stratton *Agricultural Records A.D.220 – 1977. 2nd ed.1978.*)

The most obvious difference between the two farms is that Hilltop regularly paid four men's weekly wages. These rose by oneshilling during the year, beginning in January at £5 2s. 0d. for each man.

There are no wages bills for Dale Bank in 1934 (although a man was later employed as the farm grew). Another difference is in the cost of repairs. At Hilltop the men would perhaps maintain and repair equipment; Mr Davison had to pay for that service. A wide variety of goods and services were sold from Hilltop, whilst Dale Bank's income was derived from sales of milk. It is noticeable that the largest part of Dale Bank's expenditure was on animal feed, both for cows and the working horses. Just one item, the year's supply of bran, cost over £21.

Dale Bank

Feb	12cwt bran @ 6/6d	Total £3 18s
May	4 cwt @ 5/9d	£1 14s 6d
June	5 cwt @ 3/6d	£1 7s 6d
July	5 cwt @ 5/6d,	£1 6s 6d
August	6 cwt @ 8/3d	£1 4s 9d
September	8 cwt @ 6/9d	£2 14s 0d
Oct	8 cwt @ 7/6d	£3. 0s 0d
November	8 cwt @ 7/6d	£3. 0s 0d
December	8 cwt @ 7/6d	£3. 0s 0d

Dale Bank accounts also record work on the horses' shoes.

It appears that the firm of Halksworth at Holymoorside was the main supplier of animal feeds to Hilltop Farm. There are records for most months in 1931 of payments to Halksworth, although nothing is recorded for 1934. Neither are there any blacksmiths' bills (although in April of that year, two curry combs and one dandy brush, costing three shillings altogether were bought).

For Dale Bank Farm, **January** was the time for settling the half-yearly bill from T Willmot, the Milltown blacksmith

MILLTOWN, ASHOVER,

January 1st 1934

Mr. B. Davison

DR. TO T. W. WILLMOT,
SHOEING & GENERAL SMITH.

1933		£	s	d
July 3.	Stand cep to wheel, handle to churn		1	6
Aug 14	4 new shoes		4	.
	Irons put on Breast pole, fork shafted		1	.
Sep 28.	1 knife laid, 1 pin		2	-
Oct 10.	2 old shoes		2	-
16.	1 set screw			6
Dec 7.	2 new shoes, 2 removes		5	.
15.	Fire bonnett		1	6
		£1	0	6

Paid Feb 14th 1934.
T. W. Willmot.
With Thanks.

The animal feed bills (from A Johnson, Darley Dale and J H White, Clay Cross) amounted to £15 18s. 6d. altogether. There was also a bill from the Ashover Threshing Company Limited, for £2 for threshing and 15s. for chopping. They were threshing at Hilltop too. 18s.3d. was the cost of the threshing coal, the threshing men's wages were £1 5s 0d and the Ashover butcher, Swift, was paid 13s.11d. for providing "threshing meat."

The threshing at Dale Bank was done with the aid of the Ashover Threshing Company. Farmers who subscribed to this could hire the threshing machine and other, nearby farmers would come and help. They would be unpaid (unlike the men at Hilltop) but the farmer's wife would provide the necessary food and drink. The machine would move from farm to farm and the farmers would follow it, to provide the labour force.

The only other item of expenditure at Dale Bank was for seeds from Gartons of Warrington. At Hilltop which mainly balanced the bills by sales of eggs, milk and cream, some income came from selling used potato bags (2s.6d) and from "Mrs Windle for summering two beasts" (£3 10s.).

Besides the regular wages paid at Hilltop, in **February** John Windle received 5s. for one day's work. They sold Bert Edge a calf for £1 5s., Frank Bennet a bull calf for £1 4s., and E Brocklehurst "sheep and cow" for £5 15s. As they did each month, they bought "soap and vim for churn cleaning" (2s. 6d). This was done by Mrs Barbara Bark (neé Rickers) who was then a school girl. "I used to go to Miss Bassett's at the farm, wash all their milk churns and put 'em in the sterilizer. I should be about ten." At Dale Bank the total feed bill came to £17 14s. 3d. The only other expenditure was for oats and "mangel" seed from Gartons Ltd.

In **March** more corn than in January was threshed at Hilltop, for the load of coal cost £1 1s. 6d. and seven men were paid 6s. each (£2 2s. 0d). John Windle had 10s. for walling. Mr Huckle bought a load of manure at 6s. At Dale Bank the feed bill was large at £25 9s. 9d. and a bill from T Gibson for fertilizer was £6 13s. 6d. Mrs Davison kept a large flock of hens. Two stone of layers pullets (included in the feed bill) cost 2s.6d.

April's bills for Dale Bank show that 24 stone of pig meal cost £1 1s. 9d. 40 cwt of agricultural salt was £4 0s. 0d. The mole catcher's bill reflects the difference in size between the two farms. Hilltop paid Mr Allwood 9s. at 1d. per acre. In March he had charged Dale Bank 3s.4d. (for 40 acres). That Hilltop was more than just a working farm is shown by a bill for 5s. for "Pentrich Horse Society groom fee". They received 5s. for use of Bull ..... and Mr Bagshaw paid them 10s. "for use of mare".

Fertilisers were still being ordered in **May** on Dale Bank Farm. The Clay Cross Company supplied one ton of lime dust and slag was bought from T Gibson. Hilltop paid 9s. for 14 geese eggs. The entry fee for the Blue Albion Society was paid (7s. 6d) John Windle received 6s. for wall building and Abbot, "for bringing pig" also had 6s.. For "one week's keep for pig", E Brailsford was paid 3s.6d., and he had 5s. for use of boar".

The **June** feed bill for Dale Bank was much reduced, being £6 5s. 9d. The only additional item was for the fertilizer nitro chalk (£1 4s. 0d). Hilltop Farm paid John Windle 5s. "for night work". The account book does not specify what the night work was. As usual, they balanced their outgoings with milk, eggs and cream and besides that, they sold W T Parker a mare (£29).

In **July** Dale Bank Farm received Mr Willmot's half yearly bill (for 17s.) Hilltop Farm's accounts reflect the season. John Windle who was an extra hand was paid 12s. on 7 July and 10s. on 21 July for hay making. Extra harvest food and drink cost £1. "Jim was paid 10s. "for show expence" a typical summertime item. The four weeks' wages (coming to £20 10s. were the largest part of the month's expenditure (of £27 0s. 5d).

The harvest was being gathered in at Hilltop in **August**. John Windle was paid for mowing round the cornfields and for carting and stacking the corn. The harvest beer, which came from Offilers Brewery cost £1 10s. The subscription to Bakewell Show (10s.) was paid and medicine (Monsol fluid) at 5s.6d was bought from Leonard Smith. Against their out-goings, they sent to Swift the butcher, six lambs and a calf, receiving £14 2s. 6d. Two smaller items of income were the sale of "empty bags for 6s." and "from Show Caterers for Milk 3s.9d." Dale Bank spent only on feed bills this month.

September was threshing time at Hilltop. The coal was 18s.10d the men's wages: "6 men at 6 shilling each" were £1 16s. and the "Threshing meat" was 13s. H Hole fetched "calves from Matlock Station" for 2s.6d and, perhaps because they were busy, John Windle was paid 2s.6d for milking. 2s.9d. paid for a hundredweight of poultry grit is a reminder that it was a mixed farm. Again, this month, Dale Bank paid for animal feed and the only other item was for unspecified seeds.

At Dale Bank **October** brought the annual fee payable to Greenhill Lane, Riddings and District Ploughing and Hedge Cutting Association. A cart collar, breech and crupper all needed repairing. W. Yeomans charged 10s. for this work. The bill from the Estate Office at Chatsworth for summering Mr Davison's beasts was £9 12s. 6d. At Hilltop they were able to perform this service (for H. Taylor) charging £7 14s. for five beasts. They paid R. Bagshaw for harvesting in the previous month, and E. Brailsford 15s. "for use of corn drill" R. Abbot had £1 10s. "for "takeing" two cows to Derby and one back". They bought 6d. worth of caster oil "for calves" from Mr Crossland in the village. They sold an old float to the scrapman and two "cockrills" to J. Tomlinson for 6s.

In **November** the only outgoings for Dale Bank Farm were for animal feed. Hilltop Farm paid the entry fee and transfers for the Blue Albion Society. This was 12s.6d. Two halter shanks cost 1s.

They sold E. Brocklehurst a cow and calf, for which they received 16s. For allowing Y. Young "use of Bull" they had 5s.

In **December**, seasonably they sold "20 old fowls (for £1 10s.) and "four cockrills" (for 16s.), whilst they bought "12 pullets" (for £2). Their Bull licence had to be renewed, this cost 5s. It was an expensive month for Dale Bank Farm. The vet, G. J. Furness of Alfreton sent his yearly bill. This shows that there were sheep on the farm – that the bull had warts removed (10s.6d) and the wounds dressed (8s.) and that a cow needed its rumen punctured with a trocar. G.T.Robinson, wheelwright and undertaker, of Tupton also sent his bill for the year. He had made a new oak frame for the sack barrow (8s). The horse hoe had been repaired with one ash bent side and one spender bar and one bolt. The cost of fixing was included and the total for this item was 6s.6d. A new pig form was made (with an ash top and oak legs). That cost 16s. six and three quarters of paint was mixed (4s. 6d) and a new cambrill (costing 2s. 6d) was made.

Looked at over a longer time span (that is from 1921 – 1939) the accounts give an insight into agricultural work, and, in the case of

Sayles butcher's shop.

Dale Bank Farm, an understanding of the farmer's methods. They show the equipment needed, the services that had to be paid for and the varied nature of the firms who supplied goods. The farms also sold produce. There are details too of the wages not only of agricultural workers, but of men working in associated crafts.

Bassets sold such varied items as a "Dressed goose" to Swift the butchers for 12s. 6d in December 1926 and Wool for £11 15s. in June 1928. There is no record of the purchasers. In September 1933, Sayles (another butcher in Ashover) paid £6 15s. for one sheep and two lambs and in November of that year, Swift paid half price for a lame pig. They also sold an old turnip drill in 1935 for £1 and in that same year they had a special reason for selling some milk (for 15s.) That was for a King George V. Jubilee Tea and Dance.

Swift the butcher paid them £1 10s. in December 1926 for ten weeks' keep for five lambs and Frank Bennett had had the use of one of their fields for 10s. in 1933. W. Shaw had borrowed the dipping tub (1924) and in March 1927 G. Hellaby had used their slag drill, for which they had charged him 8s. They ground corn – eight stone for C. Hollingsworth (at 1/-) and three hundreweight for 3s. for W. Taylor.

They paid for various services and these give a picture of life on the farm. A. Abbot took "Old Blossom" at the end of her working

Blossom and Bonny in 1926.

life in 1932 for £3. John Windle was paid 10d. "for thacking corn stack" in October 1931. Four years later he received 8s. "for thistle mowing". Mrs Walker was paid 1s.6d for "sitting eggs" (1933) and for "turkey mating" J. Woodward had 3s. Mr Bingham had dipped 60 sheep for which he was paid 5s. (in October 1922). A colt was castrated by R. Rollins in May 1922 for 15s. That the farm depended on horses is shown by an entry in the Account Book for September 1927. W. Taylor was paid £2 8s. 0d. for "binding 8 acres of corn with horses at 8s. an acre."

Inevitably the wages bill rose. In 1921 one man's weekly wage was £3 10s. 0d. In 1936 it was £5 6s. 0d. Four men were each paid a day's wage of 5s. in July 1922 and the rate was not increased for "Sunday work" in August 1924, or for "night work" in June of that year. J. Flint had 3s. for "mowing round fields" in August 1924 and for another seasonal job in August 1936, "Boys" (how many is not known) were paid 8s. "for weeding turnips".

In the late 1920s Bernard Davison moved from Demonsdale Farm to Dale Bank Farm. While he farmed Demonsdale he bought several big items of equipment that he needed when he was setting up in farming on his own. He bought a Number One Diamond Milk Refrigerator from T. Grayson in 1925 which cost £4 15s. and two 15 gallon milk churns besides a swath turner and a mowing machine (£27 0s. 0d).

At Dale Bank too, there were large bills, for a Dutch Barn for example. Farm sales were useful. From one, in 1930, he bought a binder for £9 5s. 0d. and a horse hoe (5s.) came, through Richardson and Linnell, auctioneers, from a similar source. Probably a more modest item, a seed hopper, did too. That cost 6d. but it was replaced in 1939 by a new one (9s.9d). That this was a new farm for Mr Davison is reflected in a bill from W. S. Burkitt, seed merchant, for 1927. This listed:

7lb single cut cow grass @ 2s.6d	17s.6d
3lb cow grass G Hybrid @ 1s.9d	5s.3d
4lb red clover @ 1s.6d	6s.
10lb White clover and alsike[1] @ 1s.9d	17s.d
3lb trefoil @ 10d	2s.6d
11lb Timothy @ 8d	7s.4d
7ld cocksfort @ 1s.3d	8s.9d
3lb Meadow fescue @ 1s.8d	5s.
21lb Italian Rye Grass @ 8d	14s.
31lb Perennial Rye Grass @ 9d	£1 3s. 3d
3lb Sheep Fescue @ 1s.6d	4s.6d
3lb Luceme @ 1s.9d	5s.3d
and 1lb Marrow Stem Kale	4s.

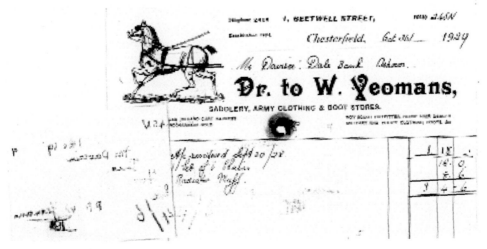

[1] Alsike is a type of clover.

The radiator muff would be for the car at that point – for a bull-nosed Morris. It hooked on the top and there were fasteners round the side to get it to warm up faster. Old tractors had radiator blinds. They ran on paraffin but you started them on petrol. So you pulled the blind down over the radiator, till it got to practically boiling point, and then the engine would be hot enough to run on paraffin. Paraffin was about half the price of petrol. The muff surface was thin leather. It was all padded inside. There were little sections on press studs, that you could lift up, to allow a certain amount of air to go through. If it was very frosty, they'd leave the muff on and perhaps if the engine was getting too hot, they'd open these flaps. They left the muff on while they were working, if it was very cold.

"I can remember it ever so plain – I should only be six or seven. It was black – a temperature gauge stuck out of the top of the radiator and the muff hooked over that. The one mentioned cost 8s.6d – from Yeomans – they probably would have made it." adds Howard.

Hemp rope was bought and a second-hand sheep rack for £5 from W. T. Parker. There were regular bills from Leonard Smith, Veterinary Chemists, that for 19 September 1925 being typical it included three bottles of Udderdyne, one bottle Woodhalls Oils (1s.6d.) One Red Drought (3s.), One tin Black Empire Compo (2.6d).

The sale of sacks gives an interesting insight into the economic conditions. For "Meal Bags returned in good condition", Roger Bower paid 3d. each and "2d. each for Robson's Cake Bags." This was in November 1929. A note attached to Roger Bower's bill for fourth April 1930, however, stated, "Sacks having been affected by the slump in Corn Prices we are now allowing 2s.3d per dozen (ordinary size) and 1s.9d. per dozen for Robson's sacks."

There were often bills for repairs showing the enormous amount of work needed to keep equipment useable. A bill for repairing and painting the Float was received in 1927 from G. Robinson (the wheelwright and undertaker of Tupton). Henry Meller, the Littlemoor carpenter, altered the dray. His bill gives an interesting detail of the labour costs. The first item reads, "To making new side board and painting – 28 hours @ 1s.6d.: - £1 14s. 0d. and "making Back Gormer and Best Gormer (this was the front gormer) for

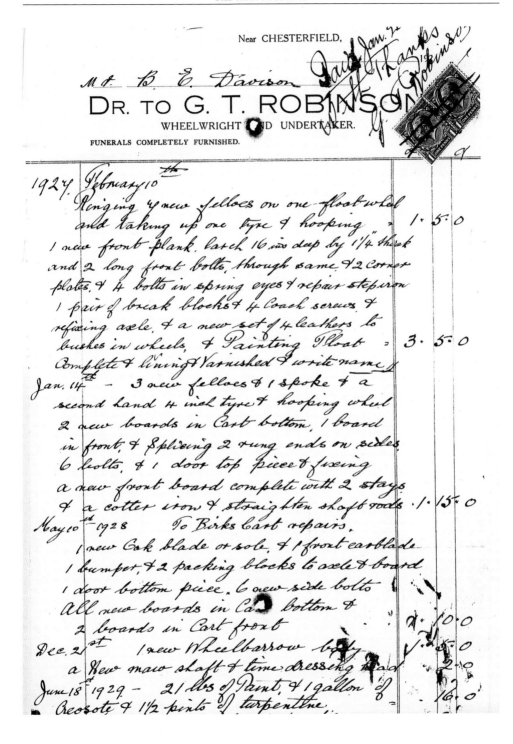

Near CHESTERFIELD,

M# B. E. Davison

DR. TO G. T. ROBINSON
WHEELWRIGHT AND UNDERTAKER.
FUNERALS COMPLETELY FURNISHED.

1924. February 10th

Ringing 4 new felloes on one float whel
and taking up one tyre & hooping — 1 . 5 . 0
1 new front plank. larch 16 ins deep by 1¼" thick
and 2 long front bolts, through same & 2 corner
plates, & 4 bolts in spring eyes & repair step iron
1 pair of break blocks & 4 Coach screws, &
refixing axle, & a new set of 4 leathers to
bushes in wheels, & Painting Float — 3 . 5 . 0
Complete & lining & Varnished & write name

Jan. 14th — 3 new felloes & 1 spoke & a
second hand 4 inch tyre & hooping wheel
2 new boards in Cart bottom, 1 board
in front, & splicing 2 rung ends on sides,
6 bolts, & 1 door top piece & fixing
a new front board complete with 2 stays
& a cotter iron & straighten shaft rods · 1 . 15 . 0

May 10th 1928   To Birks Cart repairs.
1 new Oak blade or sole, & 1 front earblade
1 bumper, & 2 packing blocks to axle & board
1 door bottom piece. 6 new side bolts
All new boards in Cart bottom &
2 boards in Cart front   . 10 . 0

Dec. 21st   1 new Wheelbarrow body
a New man shaft & time dressing   . 2 . 0

June 18th 1929 — 21 lbs of Paint, & 1 gallon of
Creosote & 1½ pints of turpentine,   . 16 . 0

same "entailed 18 Hours @ 1s.6d.: - £1 7s. 0d." Repairs to the horse-drawn machinery were made by W. Yeomans of Chesterfield. In 1938, for example, they repaired "three Binder canvasses with canvas, laths and patching same £1 7s. 0d."

Amongst various items of repair done by T. Willmot, the Milltown blacksmith, is listed an "ear" and "new ear braid". The December bill from G. Robinson includes a Christmas present. Bernard Davison's son Howard, who was six years old received "1 new wheelbarrow complete painted – for boy." Its cost – 12s.6d.

The accounts give a fascinating insight into the workings of the two farms. They reflect the huge amount of physical labour involved and the methods of working. The prices of goods and services reveal much of interest. In particular, Hilltop, in showing the prices of such things as milk and eggs, as well as the workers' wages, allows the reader a little glimpse into the standard of living.

TED HELLABY'S DIARY

Ted Hellaby who farmed in Littlemoor kept diaries for several years. This chapter uses extracts from his 1931 diary. In it he records the work on the farm and makes observations about the weather. He notes too the preachers and special services at the Methodist chapel, the local election and other incidents which interest him. Occasionally, when he felt inclined, he enlivened the entries with little pen and ink sketches.

His was mainly an arable farm but he also kept sheep. Some appeared at the Show, other, less priveleged ones came to a sad but inevitable end.

2 March 1931. Fat lambs gone to Swift's.

Other entries mark events in the life of the sheep.

17 February 1931. " Snow storms. Fastened ewes up in paddock building tonight."

The first lamb arrived on 5 March and the last on 25 April.

On 8 February he was preparing for winter threshing. The diary entry reads

" Stripped thatch off small oat stack ready for threshing. Rung R. Hinchley regarding same."

For several days, from 5-10 November he was pulling mangolds and carting them. On 10 November when all the roots had been pulled he notes the total carted as

" Twenty four loads of mangolds. Sixteen loads of turnips.

The diary also gives a glimpse of working methods.

> 16 June Rolled mangolds with Monty (the horse)
> 12 August Commenced mowing Lints in ten shilling field with sycthe.

The diary reflects too the aim that work should be thorough and that the farm should <u>appear</u> neat.

> 22 September Completed trimming oat stack.

Only on Christmas Day is there a general holiday.

Occasionally he notes prices as on

> 20 May Took stock to Bakewell. Pattie £11. Daisy and Sadie £26.

28 December was the "coldest day on record." There had previously been "Heavy snow from Friday till Saturday noon. (Milk lorry failed to collect.)" The weather might be disruptive also in summer time. Then it would be possible to catch up on odd jobs inside. On a wet day in August the cow shed was white-washed.

Spring days were not always to be relied on. On 18 April it was "snowing strong" so that "horses lay up."

Besides the Sunday services there was a "Lecture at Chapel" on Monday, 9 November and 27 October was

> "Election Day at Ashover. Rode down with Enos Lee to vote for Jacob."

A topical story occured in November. Disturbed by the festivities on bonfire night a "stray dog come."

Fortunately the entry for 11 November is

> "Stray dog claimed."

The diary gives an extra dimension and richness to the life and work of the farm as recorded in this book.

Thursday 5   (309-56)

Fine day. Pulling mangolds this morning. Carted 5 loads off this afternoon. Bon-fire night — Stray dog come.

Friday 6   (310-55)

REFLECTIONS

Farmers in this area had always grown some crops to feed their animals, but arable farming became increasingly necessary as, with war conditions, the country sought to become self sufficient in producing food. These small farms, adapting to the changing conditions, found themselves more valued and became more prosperous and efficient. Even so, on little farms the income they raised had sometimes to be supplemented with an extra job away from the farm and for the farm workers, as John Heathcote says, the wages were not good.

"When I left farming, £6.5 shillings a week was a full week's wage, and that were working like, you milked 7 days a week, twice a day, and all lot and you didn't get nowt extra. And I went to the Colour Works and me first week's wages were £11.10 shillings and something, that were for five and a half days. Never looked back after that".

Over a lifetime in farming, Howard has experienced many changes. The machinery which has replaced hand tools and horses has got bigger and heavier and more complicated.

"Most of the tractors nowadays, you can't repair them yourself, because they're all electronic gadgets on them and they're beyond us altogether. If anything goes wrong, you've got to be prepared to pay £500, £800, £1,000 out for a new part to be put in.

And besides, they're a lot heavier than they used to be. These slurry tankers for instance, they hold a thousand gallons and the tanker itself, when it's empty, could weigh three tons or so. You've perhaps seven or eight tons in that one thing on, probably, two wheels. Admitted, they've bigger, wider tyres so the weight's spread out more. But I think they do more damage than the older, smaller machines. Get heavy

land like mine, the less you go on to it the better, they're
bound to damage the soil structure. In the old days, the little
old grey Ferguson weighed a ton. That was all it was, and its
little light implements behind it. Instead of one big huge
tractor today, they'd happen have seven or eight of these
little tractors doing the same job. But of course, they can't
afford it now. It's just got to be one man do everything."

Farming methods have changed too.
"I think perhaps the old methods were more balanced. We'd
more rotational crops in that day, it was a five year rotation.
It'd be wheat or oats, we didn't grow much barley. And then
there'd be roots. And then grass for a year and then it'd be
wheat first and then perhaps oats, roots again then there'd
happen be another wheat crop and then it'd be seeded down
to grass. It would only grow for one year, then you ploughed
it up. And that'd be the rotation. It'd give fields a rest but you
don't get that so much now. You seldom grass fields down and
there's no roots grown at all. It's all silage now. So times have
changed quite a bit. A lot of barley is grown and sold for
malting instead of just cattle feed but then they're growing
this oilseed rape as well, that's a different crop that's come on
the market. And linseed, there's not so much round here but
in arable areas they grow quite a lot of that, I think."

But the developments have not, he considers, been altogether an
improvement.
"When you look back, we seemed to enjoy life a lot better in
those days. We worked hard. It was heavy, sometimes
miserable jobs, and yet we seemed to get more pleasure out of
it. And more satisfaction at the end of the day."

Miss Lennox's high regard for the farmers echoes this,
"I always say there's no-one works so hard for so little. It's the
hardest job – and yet they're devoted to it, most of them."

"I think," Howard continues, "we seemed to be able to live
more comfortably somehow. Nowadays, you've a job to make
ends meet. And it seems just like a rat-race today."

As Eva Butler says

"They were more relaxing days. Life didn't go at a hurtling
pace – everything is rush, rush, rush now. It was hard work,
but then again, we didn't realise it was at the time, because
everybody else was doing the same thing. Like wall building
and hedge laying, people did that. Now they just have a
machine that wraps things about – leave the wall down, put
in a bit of barbed wire and make it do. They don't make half
as good a job."

October 5ᵗʰ 1977.

*Something of the laborious work and yet the tranquil surroundings is conveyed by Ted
Hellaby's picture.*

And John Heathcote considers

"That were heart of farming. Having a farm that looked
decent. A decent farm and animals that looked well and

horses that were well and a lot of farmers, they were quite happy if they'd got that. At that time I wouldn't think they were very bothered about making a lot of money so long as they paid their way and got some good animals through for folks to look at. Completely different way altogether. It were."

There is also, Howard thinks, too much interference by the government at present.

"I think life was nicer, easier. We hadn't the humbug and the paper-work and the authorities on our back that we've got now. We could do as we liked and as long as we abided by the simple rules, nobody interfered with us. We could just grow what we liked, when we liked, how we liked, and sell what we liked.

Miss Lennox agrees that the paperwork farmers now have to deal with is mountainous but, even in her working days, it was a problem:

"Farmers were always overflowing with forms to fill in – it's even worse now. They could never find the forms that I wanted without a lot of trouble. I remember one farmer saying "Come inside and see if you can find the form". There was a big desk, he opened it and the whole floor was covered – there must have been a hundred bits of paper. He said, "It won't be in that, because those are for immediate attention.""

Nowadays, Howard considers, the Government affects a farmer a lot in his day-to-day life.

"They rule us completely. We hardly own our own land, we're ordered about on everything that we grow and everything we do. It's DEFRA. Dairy farmers have inspectors nearly every week, telling them that this wants doing and that wants doing. We haven't anything that we can do without they interfere with us now. It's disheartening. I can't sell anything off my land because I'm not Farm Assured. I think the worst of the rules and regulations come in stock rearing. There's a time for spreading manure: you mustn't do it if the ground's frozen and you mustn't do it if it's water logged. And if you have a slurry store it's got to hold at least a year's supply of slurry and then you can only put that on at certain times. And only put so much on because of nitrate pollution and you mustn't spread within ten metres of a water course. Besides that, each field has to have a record of everything that's put on it – even the amount of muck that cows put on the field in summer, when they're grazing. The authorities have worked out how much muck a cow does every day and worked out the chemical analysis of it. All the rules come from Brussels now, they make all the laws there. But the French and the Italians and the Germans they don't care anything about the laws. And they get away with it.

Nothing bothered us in those days at all. We had a Dairy Inspector come round perhaps once a year. He'd just look round the buildings and see as they were reasonably clean and your dairy clean – they'd just have a look round and come in and have a cup of tea and leave us alone for another year. If anything wanted doing, he'd tell us, but that's as far as it went. But as regards growing crops we just did as we thought fit.

There wasn't much form filling: I think we'd what they called Agricultural Returns to fill in every half year. And you simply put down what crops you grew, how many cattle you'd got, how many acres of wheat and barley. You'd nothing to bother about really. You could sit down and almost do it out of your head because you knew your fields and knew your cattle. You just ticked each item off. One bit of a night and that was your form filled in for another six months. Now there's forms arriving every week. Well I can never sort out the forms, they're so complicated. You see, they've changed the whole system this year. Instead of the IACCS payment for growing corn, it's this single form payment.

At one time your product was wanted and you grew as much as you could and you were making a reasonable living out of it. But it's dwindled year by year over the last twenty years I should think. Ten years ago we were getting £120 a ton for our wheat, now we're getting £60. And we haven't a say in it, they say what they're going to give us for it. It's hardly worth growing......My wheat always went into Johnsons at Darley Dale – Just ring them up, "I've 15 tons of wheat. Can you deal with it?" They'd come on such a day and chap'd be content to sit in his lorry while I loaded, it'd happen take us a couple of hours to load it....but as time went on, he didn't want to be sitting, wasting time waiting for me filling it. They wanted it filled in quarter of an hour, then they wanted it tested for quality...There's so much bureaucracy."

The war was useful in that it brought thousands of acres into good production but now Governmental theories hamper farming practices and the public perception and understanding of the farmer is not sympathetic.

"That old pasture grass didn't grow a very thick crop and not very nourishing stuff either. When they ploughed it up, in war time, they'd got all these new grass seeds, better quality stuff and it made a lot better feed for cattle and more productive as well – it yielded a lot heaver and that's gone on every since. And now we've got to revert to the old grasses again. They don't want these nice lush pastures. We've got to seed the old wild flower mixtures back into the land and go back to the old way of growing. I don't know what it'll be like then. We've spent all this time and money improving grassland and making it good for cattle feed and now we've got to go back to the old way again.

A lot of folks don't understand it. We're getting paid now for looking after the countryside and "providing the countryside for the people to enjoy" instead of growing crops on it. So that the ramblers can come round and look at all these wild flowers growing in your fields and all the weeds growing in your corn crops and think how nice it all is.

Badgers are a pest. The trouble is, you're not allowed to cull them and they've no predators. For one thing, they're destroying all the ground nesting birds. They eat their eggs and they eat the young ones. Nobody says anything about that. They say it's farming practices that have done that. Oh, yes, it's always the rotten farmers who are to blame for everything. But nothing's said about badgers destroying the ground nesting birds and they do. These folks say, "Oh, they only eat worms and grubs". They don't keep that body up on worms and grubs; they eat something better than that....The Government won't listen. No they're not going to do anything yet. They're waiting for further developments and further tests.

Dec 31ˢᵗ 1972.

Badgers by Ted Hallaby.

And they say that now there's a lot of these sparrow hawks getting about, they're killing little birds. And there again you see, it's the rotten farmer who's destroying the little birds! And of course a lot of the public believe that because they're told, television tells it to them. Town folks, they don't know anything about farming and they just believe everything that the media tells them."

Certain smells bring powerful memories.

"There's catmint. I remember that quite well, because that used to grow quite a lot in corn crops. Aye. Because there was no weed killer in them days there'd be all sorts of weeds of various types in amongst the corn. This catmint, when you went over it, crushed it with a wheel, or even walked on it, it used to give this powerful smell of mint off, and I always remember that. There would be barley, that's a smell of its own, a very distinctive smell when it starts ripening and I can remember that. And when you mow grass, you get that smell of freshly mown grass. And then, if your hay is good hay, that's a distinctive smell as well. Good hay has a smell of its own. I can't describe that either but it's not at all compared to grass. It's a different smell entirely. And even nowadays, you get that, even in baled hay. You get it particularly in loose hay, it was ever such a distinctive smell. And even when you dug it, cut it out of the stack in winter, you'd still get it then. If it was good quality hay. But if it was bad quality hay, well it just stunk, that's the only way you can describe it. If it had had a lot of rain on it and it had gone dusty and dirty, it was a rotten smell. And cows didn't like it either. They wouldn't eat bad hay. I'm surprised that folks don't know what good hay smells like. But I mean if you're not in contact with it, you don't know, do you? You'll smell new grass, because that wafts over the wall and as you walk past it, you can smell it, when it's been newly mown. But good hay, you've got to be among it, to smell it. And you could pull a handful out of a stack and smell at it and you could tell straight away what quality it was, whether it was good or bad.

Ah, I think my favourite period in the year was harvest time. I used to enjoy that better than anything. Hay-making was manual work, but I used to enjoy it. It was nice sunny, warm, dry weather and you could go out into the fields long days, short nights and I seemed to get a lot of pleasure out of that. And I think, corn harvest, that was my favourite time. You had the satisfaction of reaping your crops. It was a sociable time too because, in those days, we should perhaps have four or five people come in and help us.

The farmer, doing his fieldwork, is looking round and seeing things altering all the time.

Several entries in Ted Hellaby's diary reflect his particular interest in bird life.

March 21ˢᵗ 1986

4 November 1931 "a huge gaggle of wild geese."
26 December "Seen kestrel hawk on Barn field."

Even today it's the same with me when I'm ploughing or anything. I'm always looking round and seeing what's happening
round about and looking what other people are doing in their
fields, or what's growing in another field. And it's not a boring
job at all. No. Even now, and although it's a one-man job, it's
not exactly lonely, because you see nature and something
interesting all the time.

We see it, but town folks don't. They don't seem to look at it
in the same light at all because they don't know about it from

the beginning. I don't know what their opinion is, but they're not brought up on it like we are. We've grown crops on it and seen animals and know it from the beginning to the end. We always know what's going to happen next, and look for it and expect something either growing or something happening. It's just a continual cycle to us. It's so varied, it's not monotonous at all. One thing will come, then it'll go and then there's something else starting to happen. It's living with nature. I know it's a lot faster way of life with machinery and that, it gets on with the job a lot quicker, but even so, when you've been brought up in it all your life you never lose it. It stops with you. I shouldn't like to be out of it."

John Heathcote missed his farming life:
"It's terrible when you give up. When you've never done nothing else. It's a big thing. There were times when you didn't know what to do wi yoursen."

Howard has no intention of giving up.
"I know I've got to go slower, I get tired. I mean, at 78 you can't expect working like you were when you were 38. But I still enjoy what I do. Look forward to – just now it's nasty cold weather and I don't like turning out in it, but I'm looking forward to it when a bit warmer weather comes and I can get out in the fields and do something and look round and see what's happening. Oh I shall keep doing it just as a hobby. I like to go out into my fields and plough and sow and reap. It's satisfying."

For the farmer, the work provides deep fulfilment. He is almost part of the land he farms. Howard is aware of the encroaching dicouragements. He will though, continue farming.

THE MAKING OF THIS BOOK.

This oral history recording project began in 2003 with the object of describing life in and around Ashover in the first part of the twentieth century through the words, thoughts and impressions of those who lived it. At first the most elderly people were interviewed, beginning with the recording of Mrs Olive Scott's memories. Two booklets, *Ashover Remembered* and *Barm and Battleships* have been published so far. As a result of their success, younger interviewees came forward and the project began to broaden geographically. Some topics, notably farming life, turned out have a general interest far beyond the confines of a single village and so the idea of this book of memories was born.

THE MEMORIES

Memory is not simple. Facts and impressions, overlaid by time and experience may be moulded, unconsciously, by a person, to become his memories. Things fade, or remain vivid, for different reasons, and a person remembers things of personal significance. Even important historical moments impact on individuals differently. Personality has an effect too. The person who is observant (and who has a lively interest in other people) retains details more readily than someone who does not have such powers of observation. In remembering, one detail might have impressed one individual, while another person might focus on a completely different aspect. Since the aim of this work was to provide a richly detailed account of how life was to those who experienced it, it was important to combine the different aspects. In this way, the fullest possible picture was obtained.

METHOD

The method of interviewing combined a mixture of direction and informality. Before any recording was started, prospective interviewees were given a general idea of the type of memories that would be useful. Once the recordings started, though, if the person appeared to be confident, he or she was free to talk uninterrupted. The interviewer's aim was to be as unobtrusive as possible. People, though, often do not realise the significance of their own lives, particularly their working lives, with their apparently "every day" routines and episodes. Sometimes a prompt was useful. This might take the form of repeating a key word or phrase in what someone had just said. This gave them the opportunity to elaborate and to describe something which might have seemed straightforward or unremarkable to them, but which, because it is now in the past is not fully understood.

Pauses were considered useful. Provided that they were not too long, they would allow the interviewee to gather his or her thoughts and then go a little deeper into previous remarks.

The tape recordings were transcribed verbatim and all these transcripts are available for inspection in the Local Studies Library, County Hall, Matlock. To compile a readable account for publication, the transcripts have been edited. Repetitions and phrases such as "you see" have been deleted, while attempting to retain the flavour of each individual's style of speech.

If you have enjoyed this book you may also like to read other oral history titles published by Derbyshire County Council Cultural & Community Services Department:

Two earlier titles featuring some of the contributors to Milk Muck and Memories:

Ashover Remembered Price £4.00 post free.
Barm and Battleships: memories of childhood in Ashover Price £5.00 including postage.

More oral histories:
Props, points and pig iron
An illustrated oral history of Renishaw.
£5.00 (£7.00 including post and packing.)

Now we're here. Voices from Chesterfield's hidden history
People of many different nationalities and cultures have made Chesterfield their home. Here 20 living historians share their life experiences.
Price: £7.99 (£10 including post and packing)

Two fascinating Victorian farmers' diaries.

A Victorian Farmer's Diary. William Hodkin's Diary 1864 to 1866
Life in and around Beeley on the Chatsworth Estate.
Price £6.95 (£8.50 including post and packing.)

Melbourne 1820-1875. A Diary by John Joseph Briggs
Briggs was a gentleman farmer. His diary is full of enthralling snippets of village life, national events, natural history and of course, the weather.
Price £4.99 (£7.00 including post and packing.)

For mail order please send a cheque payable to Derbyshire County Council to:
Derbyshire County Council
Cultural and Community Services Department
County Hall, Matlock, Derbyshire DE4 3AG